INTRODUCTION

CW01500071

What is a scene? In theater, with the excep
most scenes are interactions between two o
demonstrate the emotions, personalities, r
the characters involved. They help to re
conflicts, agreements or hidden emotions between the
characters. And they give the actors playing those characters
the opportunity to experience, explore and learn from the
choices made by the other actors in the scene. Put two or more
actors together onstage and the possibility for almost any
situation or emotion instantly comes alive – along with the
possibility for every form of human relationship, from equal to
unequal to evolving.

With that thought in mind, the thirty-four scenes contained in
this book were created to provide young actors with the
material to explore a full spectrum of age-appropriate emotions
and relationships, ranging from fear to friendship, love to
loathing, and cooperation to competition – with moments of
sadness, sympathy, silliness, envy, guilt, anger, and everything
in between.

In order to help young actors get the most from their experience,
the language used in every scene is typical everyday language,
rather than the sometimes outdated or overly poetic language
that is often found in books of scenes collected from older plays.
This emphasis on contemporary language and situations allows
the actors to focus directly on the scenes, emotions and
characters, without being distracted by unfamiliar words or
turns of phrase.

Who is This Book For?

This book was written both for young actors and for the
teachers, directors and acting coaches who work with them.
More specifically, the material in *Contemporary Scenes for Young
Actors 2* was written to be performed by actors ranging from
ages 8-16, with some of the scenes created for actors towards

the upper end of that range and some for actors toward the lower end. The scenes are presented in no particular order, allowing every actor the freedom to choose the scenes that best meet with his or her individual tastes, needs, and desire for a challenge.

A Quick Word for Actors

To add flexibility, almost any role in any scene can be played by a male or female actor. Wherever this is not true, the details will be indicated both in the table of contents and in a small note just under the scene's title.

Similarly, while most of the scenes in this book were written for two actors, there are several scenes included that were written for three actors, and one scene written for four. The number of actors in each scene is indicated both in the table of contents and directly under each scene's title.

When choosing a scene, feel free to explore at random – the individual pieces are presented in no particular order. The goal is simply to find a scene that works with your needs or that challenges your skills. In other words, you may purposely choose *not* to look for the roles or situations that are most like you or that come most easily. You may decide to deliberately choose a scene where the character is absolutely nothing like you or is experiencing an emotion that you are uncomfortable or unfamiliar with.

Finally, once you've chosen a scene, as you prepare, ask yourself a few basic questions: What is the setting? Who is your character? What is your character's relationship to the other character(s) in the scene? And – perhaps most importantly – what is your character feeling and how, when and why do those feelings change over the course of the scene?

Beyond that, just have fun!

Contemporary Scenes
for Young Actors
2

Douglas M. Parker

Published by Act One Press
Copyright © 2022 by Douglas M. Parker

All rights reserved. No part of this book may be reproduced or transmitted in any form or by any means, electronic or mechanical, including photocopying, recording or any other storage and retrieval system, without the written permission of the author or publisher.

For any form of non-amateur presentation, including but not limited to professional theater, stage, television and radio, permission must be obtained from the author or publisher.

Manufactured in the United States of America.

ISBN-13: 978-1-7340014-1-9
ISBN-10: 1-7340014-1-0

For Ruby,
and for every young actor,
age one to one-hundred.

Also by Douglas M. Parker

Contemporary Monologues for Young Actors

Fantasy Monologues for Young Actors

Contemporary Scenes for Young Actors

Contemporary Monologues for Young Actors 2

Pandemic Monologues for Young Actors

CONTENTS

INTRODUCTION iii

SCIENCE *(Scene for 2 actors)* 1

SHELTER *(Scene for 2 actors)* 3

COMPETITION *(Scene for 2 actors)* 6

NEGOTIATION *(Scene for 2 actors)* 9

NUTS *(Scene for 2 actors)* 12

DINING *(Scene for 2 actors)* 15

ESCAPE *(Scene for 2 actors)* 19

OTHER WORDS *(Scene for 2 actors)* 22

POETRY *(Scene for 3 actors)* 25

SUN *(Scene for 2 actors)* 30

FAMILY *(Scene for 2 actors)* 34

DOING TIME *(Scene for 2 actors)* 37

MODERN ART *(Scene for 2 actors)* 41

BUNKER *(Scene for 3 actors)* 45

BAND *(Scene for 2 actors)* 48

DELIVERY *(Scene for 2 actors)* 52

ENCOUNTER *(Scene for 2 actors)* 55

GO FISH *(Scene for 2 actors)* 58

DRAMA *(Scene for 2 female actors)* 62

DRAMA *(Scene for 2 male actors)* 66

CAMPING *(Scene for 2 actors)* 70

CHAT *(Scene for 2 actors)* 74

POPULAR *(Scene for 2 actors)* 77

GOSSIP *(Scene for 3 actors)* 80

TIME *(Scene for 2 actors)*   83

AFTERNOON *(Scene for 2 actors)*   86

OUTER SPACES *(Scene for 2 actors)*   89

PANIC *(Scene for 2 actors)*   92

LEMONS *(Scene for 2 actors)*   96

HEALTHY *(Scene for 2 actors)*   99

THE TRUE STORY *(Scene for 4 actors)*   104

MEET & GREET *(Scene for 1 male, one female)*   108

KNOCK KNOCK *(Scene for 2 actors)*   111

GOING UP *(Scene for 3 actors)*   115

THE END *(Scene for 2 actors)*   119

ABOUT THE AUTHOR   126

SCENES

SCIENCE

(Scene for two people.)

(BLAIR and KELLY are making a presentation in science class.)

BLAIR: So, for our science project today we decided to investigate why are all little brothers so annoying?

KELLY: Is it because they want to be?

BLAIR: Or because they can't help themselves?

KELLY: A fascinating question, and one worthy of investigation.

BLAIR: We began by simply asking both our little brothers, why are you so annoying?

KELLY: Interestingly, they both gave the exact same answer – "No, you are."

BLAIR: Which was not helpful, but which did prove the universality of every little brother being annoying.

KELLY: Often in the exact same way.

BLAIR: To dig a little deeper, we then tried an experiment.

KELLY: If little brothers are annoying simply because they want to be, that would mean they could actually stop being annoying if they decided to.

BLAIR: To test this possibility, we offered each of our little brothers five dollars to not be annoying for a whole hour.

KELLY: Mine said OK, but then insisted on being paid

1

before we started. Since I didn't trust him to give me back the five dollars if he didn't last for an hour, that part of the experiment ended really quickly and completely inconclusively.

BLAIR: My little brother also said OK, but then we almost immediately got into a fight about whether him looking at me counted as him being annoying or not.

KELLY: Science is hard.

BLAIR: Totally. Also, I wasn't able to conduct any additional experiments on my little brother, because my mom heard us arguing and told us no desserts for a week if we didn't both go to our rooms like right now.

KELLY: My experiment incurred a similar outcome when my mom also heard *me* and *my* little brother fighting about who was more annoying. Except that my experiment also included me not getting any allowance for the next two weeks for talking back.

BLAIR: So in conclusion, although we were unable to determine exactly *why* all little brothers are annoying, we were absolutely able to confirm that they totally are. Right?

KELLY: Totally.

BLAIR: And that concludes our presentation. Thank you.

– END SCENE –

SHELTER

(Scene for two people.)

(CASEY and DALE are standing under a tree, sheltering from a rainstorm.)

CASEY: *(Looking up at the sky.)* What do you think?

DALE: *(Looking up.)* I don't know.

CASEY: Like five more minutes?

DALE: Maybe. But probably more.

CASEY: Yeah. *(Looking at the sky.)* A lot more.

DALE: Hours more.

CASEY: Maybe days.

DALE: Or weeks.

CASEY: I mean, it's got to stop raining sometime.

DALE: But what if it's not for, like, a whole week? Could we survive here?

CASEY: *(Thinking.)* Well, I've got Cheetos in my bookbag.

DALE: *(Pulling gum out of pocket.)* I have gum.

CASEY: Gum's not food.

DALE: It is if you swallow it.

CASEY: I guess.

DALE: *(Looking at the sky.)* And we got plenty of water.

CASEY: *(Looking at the sky.)* A *lot* of water.

DALE: Too much water.

CASEY: Dude, I would totally trade some of this water for more Cheetos.

DALE: And I would trade those extra Cheetos for a bunch of pizza.

CASEY: Plus a TV.

DALE: Plus a ride home.

CASEY: Totally. I mean we wouldn't even *need* a TV here if we had a ride home. We both have TVs in our houses.

DALE: We also have cookies at my house.

CASEY: We've got Hot Pockets.

DALE: Oh dude, if I had some Hot Pockets right now, I really couldn't care less about Cheetos. Or even cookies. I really like Hot Pockets.

CASEY: Yeah, me too.

> *(BOTH stand for an extended moment, thinking their own thoughts and looking at the sky.)*

DALE: It's not going to stop raining in five minutes is it?

CASEY: Not even in ten.

DALE: There's only one way to get those Hot Pockets.

CASEY: I know.

(CASEY and DALE look at each other for a moment.)

DALE: Ready?

CASEY: Go!

(CASEY and DALE sprint offstage.)

– END SCENE –

COMPETITION

(Scene for two people.)

(BRETT and RILEY are talking about an animal on the ground in front of them.)

BRETT: No, she loves me more.

RILEY: No, she loves me more.

BRETT: She just pretends to love you because you feed her.

RILEY: Nuh unh.

BRETT: Uh huh.

RILEY: Well, you feed her too.

BRETT: Just because I know she loves me and she's telling me she's hungry. It's not like a bribe or anything – like with some people around here.

RILEY: You think I'm *bribing* her?

BRETT: What else would you call it when you throw food at her and say, "You love me. Yes you do. You really, really love me."

RILEY: Well at least I'm not making goo-goo noises.

BRETT: Goo-goo noises?

RILEY: *(Imitating Brett.)* "Who's Brett's little monster? Goo-goo-goo. Who's Brett's favorite little monster? Goo-goo-goo-goo."

BRETT: You just don't understand us. *(To the "little monster.")*

Isn't that right little monster? Goo-goo-goo-goo-goo.

RILEY: She isn't even looking at you. She's looking at me.

BRETT: That's because you're making a scene. She's
embarrassed for you.

RILEY: Is not.

BRETT: So totally is.

RILEY: OK then, let's have a contest. No food. We'll just call
her and see who she comes to, OK?

BRETT: Fine.

RILEY: Here little girl, come here.

BRETT: Come on, little monster. Goo-goo-goo-goo-goo.

RILEY: Seriously? Again with the goo-goo?

BRETT: You'll see. Come on monster!

RILEY: Over here girl! Come on!

BRETT: Goo-goo-goo-goo.

RILEY: Here girl!

(BOTH stop calling and wait for a moment.)

BRETT: This isn't working.

RILEY: I think she's walking away.

BRETT: Definitely walking away.

RILEY: Come on girl!

BRETT: Here monster!

(BOTH stop calling and wait for a moment.)

RILEY: I don't think she loves either of us.

BRETT: Me neither.

RILEY: It's so hard to tell with pigeons.

BRETT: Right?

RILEY: You know what? Forget her. Let's go feed the ducks.

BRETT: Definitely.

(RILEY and BRETT start to exit.)

RILEY: *(Turning back to talk to the pigeon while continuing to exit.)* At least *someone* appreciates us.

(RILEY and BRETT exit.)

– END SCENE –

NEGOTIATION

(Scene for two people.)

(JESS and TRACY are outside in the schoolyard. They each have a paper bag with their lunch in it. It's lunchtime.)

JESS: *(Looking inside paper bag.)* What did you get today?

TRACY: *(Looking inside paper bag and pulling out a sandwich. Happily.)* Ohh. My mom made me bacon, lettuce and tomato. What did you get?

JESS: *(Pulling out sandwich.)* Peanut butter and jelly.

TRACY: Didn't she make that yesterday?

JESS: And the day before. And the day before that.

TRACY: Hunh.

JESS: I'll trade you half a PB&J for half a bacon, lettuce and tomato.

TRACY: Half a PB&J for a quarter of a bacon, lettuce and tomato.

JESS: That's not fair.

TRACY: Bacon, lettuce and tomato is better than peanut butter and jelly, so it's worth more.

JESS: Who says a BLT is better?

TRACY: You did, when you saw it and said you wanted to trade.

JESS: Well, maybe I think they're equal.

TRACY: Great. Then you'll be equally happy not trading.

JESS: *(Pulling out a bag of M&M's. Annoyed.)* OK. Fine. Half a peanut butter and jelly, plus ten M&M's for a half a BLT.

TRACY: I have a better idea.

JESS: What. Plus fifteen M&M's?

TRACY: Nope.

JESS: Plus *twenty*? Argh. I am so sick of peanut butter and jelly.

TRACY: I am too.

JESS: What are you talking about? Your mom *never* makes PB&J.

TRACY: You know I ate half your sandwich yesterday. And the day before. And I think the day before that.

JESS: I guess.

(BOTH think for a moment.)

TRACY: What's the cafeteria lunch today?

JESS: How should I know?

TRACY: What day is it?

JESS: Thursday.

(JESS and TRACY suddenly look at each other.)

TRACY & JESS: *(Simultaneously.)* Pizza day!

JESS: Let's do it!

TRACY: I'm in. Let's just leave the lunches here.

> *(JESS and TRACY get up and start to exit, leaving the lunches behind.)*

JESS: Why do you always have to bargain like that?

TRACY: I didn't even care about the M&M's. I'm just so tired of your mom's peanut butter and jelly.

JESS: I get it.

TRACY: And now neither of us has to eat it!

JESS: Go pizza!

TRACY & JESS: *(Simultaneously.)* Goooo pizza!

> *(JESS and TRACY exit.)*

– END SCENE –

NUTS

(Scene for two people.)

> *(At start, two squirrels, SHAWN and DYLAN, are sitting on their haunches with their paws lifted up in front of their chests in squirrel position.)*

SHAWN: Being a squirrel is hard.

DYLAN: You don't know that.

SHAWN: Of course I do. I *am* a squirrel.

DYLAN: Yeah, but you've never been anything *but* a squirrel. For all you know, being a squirrel is actually the *easiest* thing to be.

SHAWN: I don't know. What about the whole gathering nuts for winter thing? That's not easy.

DYLAN: Seriously? The nuts fall off the trees. You pick them up off the ground and hide them somewhere. What's so hard about that?

SHAWN: I think it's the uncertainty.

DYLAN: What uncertainty?

SHAWN: OK, like, what are we gathering the nuts *for*?

DYLAN: Because we need enough food to get through till spring.

SHAWN: Right. Now you're getting it.

> *(Looks at Dylan for a moment, frowning.)*
DYLAN: Getting what?

12

SHAWN: Look at me . . . What if spring never comes and we're doing this for nothing?

DYLAN: Dude, that's crazy talk. Spring always comes.

SHAWN: No it doesn't. Spring doesn't come in winter.

DYLAN: No, but . . .

SHAWN: And spring doesn't come in summer, or in the fall. How can you say something always comes when actually it almost never comes?

DYLAN: Wow. Talk about nuts. Do you have thoughts like that all the time?

SHAWN: Pretty much.

DYLAN: Do you *like* thinking thoughts like that?

SHAWN: I mean, not really.

DYLAN: Huh. You know what would take your mind off those thoughts?

SHAWN: What?

DYLAN: Collecting nuts . . . Seriously. If you really get into it, the more nuts you get, the less nuts you feel. It's like the first rule of being a squirrel. You just have to make it into a game.

SHAWN: Really?

DYLAN: Try it.

> (SHAWN *picks a nut up off the ground and looks at it.*)

SHAWN: Huh.

DYLAN: Now pick up another one. *(SHAWN picks up another nut and starts to smile.)* Now you have *two*! How does that feel?

SHAWN: It feels pretty good, actually. Look! There's another one over there. *(SHAWN picks up another nut.)* And there! *(SHAWN picks up another nut and starts excitedly looking around for more.)*

DYLAN: OK, whoever gets the most nuts wins. Go!

SHAWN: *(Picking up a nut.)* Got one!

DYLAN: *(Picking up a nut.)* Got one!

SHAWN : *(Picking up a nut.)* Got one!

DYLAN: *(Picking up a nut.)* Got one!

SHAWN: You know what? Maybe being a squirrel isn't so bad.

DYLAN: Told ya so.

SHAWN: *(Picking up a nut.)* Hah! *(SHAWN stares at the nut for a moment, then looks over at Dylan and smiles.)* Totally nuts!

DYLAN
Yeah!

– END SCENE –

DINING

(Scene for two people.)

(Siblings ALEX and CAMERON are standing in the kitchen. On the counter in front of them is an open cookbook.)

ALEX: Are you sure you want to do this?

CAMERON: Dude, totally. For all we know we're gonna grow up to be the two greatest chefs in the city.

ALEX: Or the state.

CAMERON: Maybe the country.

ALEX: Even the universe! *(ALEX and CAMERON look at each other.)* OK, the city.

CAMERON: Yeah, totally the city.

ALEX: OK, let's just read the directions first. What does the cookbook say?

CAMERON: It says, "In mixing bowl, whisk four eggs."

ALEX: Do you think a mixing bowl is different from a regular bowl?

CAMERON: No idea. And what does whisk mean?

ALEX: No idea.

CAMERON: OK, we'll just crack four eggs into a bowl.

ALEX: Cool.

CAMERON: Go to the next direction.

ALEX: *(Reading from cookbook.)* Add two tablespoons whole milk.

CAMERON: So, two tablespoons, or the whole milk?

ALEX: Let's split the difference. We'll add half the milk.

CAMERON: Smart. Then what?

ALEX: *(Reading from cookbook.)* Place one tablespoon butter in pre-heated skillet –

CAMERON: Stop. Skillet?

ALEX: Maybe . . . pot?

CAMERON: Yeah. Pot.

ALEX: That's the only thing that would hold half a gallon of milk and four eggs anyway.

CAMERON: We got this.

ALEX: *(Reading from cookbook.)* Pour contents of bowl into skillet.

CAMERON: That part sounds easy.

ALEX: Totally. *(Reading from cookbook.)* Using spatula, continuously fold eggs until curds are medium firm.

CAMERON: *What?*

ALEX: Spatula?

CAMERON: Curd?

ALEX: Is this recipe even in English?

CAMERON: And how could anyone fold an egg?

ALEX: This doesn't make any sense.

CAMERON: Go to the next direction.

ALEX: *(Reading from cookbook.)* Using spatula, continuously fold eggs until curds are medium firm.

CAMERON: No, the next direction.

ALEX: There is no next direction.

>*(ALEX and CAMERON look at each other.)*

CAMERON: Urghhh. We are *never* gonna be the best chefs in the universe.

ALEX: Or the state.

CAMERON: Or even the city.

ALEX: So what should we do?

>*(ALEX and CAMERON look at each other.)*

BOTH: *(Simultaneously looking stage left and yelling to another part of the house.)* MOM!

CAMERON: Mom!

ALEX: Mom!

CAMERON: Can you make us some scrambled eggs?

ALEX: *(To Cameron.)* That'll work.

CAMERON: Totally. And after breakfast, we can figure out something else to be the best in the world at.

ALEX: Deal.

BOTH: *(Simultaneously looking stage left and yelling to another part of the house.)* MOM!

– END SCENE –

ESCAPE

(Scene for two people.)

(QUINN and TJ are sitting at their desks in class. BOTH look expressionlessly towards the front of the classroom. After several moments, TJ speaks.)

TJ: This is boring.

QUINN: So boring.

TJ: Brandon wouldn't know how to give a book report if it was on a book about giving book reports.

QUINN: But he just keeps on trying.

TJ: Want to know how bored I am? I'm as bored the chairman of the board.

QUINN: I'm as bored as a wooden board.

TJ: I'm as bored as a chalk board.

QUINN: I'm as bored as . . . I don't even know what, but really, really bored.

TJ: We should escape and do something fun.

QUINN: Let's just run out the door and go up to the park.

TJ: Or climb out the window and go down to the river.

QUINN: Or dig a tunnel from the basement and . . . then . . . go . . . skydiving. *(TJ looks at QUINN questioningly.)* I don't know.

TJ: The point is, no one could stop us.

QUINN: Yeah. Like how? Tackle us?

TJ: The door is right there.

QUINN: We're practically touching it.

TJ: But what about . . . ?

QUINN : What?

TJ: I mean, isn't today the soccer tryouts?

QUINN: . . . I guess . . . And it is kinda cold out.

TJ: Maybe even windy.

QUINN: Definitely windy.

TJ: Might rain later.

QUINN: Probably.

TJ: So should we stay?

QUINN : Just for today. Tomorrow we will definitely dig
  a tunnel from the basement and then go skydiving.

TJ: Definitely.

> *(BOTH turn and pay attention to the person giving
> a book report for a few moments.)*

QUINN: Still boring.

TJ: So boring.

QUINN: As boring as a wild boar.

TJ: What?

QUINN : The animal. Like a wild pig.

TJ: Oh yeah. Good one.

> *(QUINN and TJ turn and watch the book report for a moment, then simultaneously heave a big sigh.)*

– END SCENE –

OTHER WORDS

(Scene for two people.)

(At start, JAMIE is sitting alone. After a moment, TAYLOR enters.)

TAYLOR: Hey.

JAMIE: Go away.

TAYLOR: Just listen.

JAMIE: Go. Away. Why do you have to be that way?

TAYLOR: I know.

JAMIE: I mean, the things you say sometimes.

TAYLOR: I know.

JAMIE: You really can be –

TAYLOR: *(Cutting JAMIE off.)* I *know*. I just want to say . . .

(TAYLOR hesitates.)

JAMIE: Yeah?

TAYLOR: I just want to say . . .

JAMIE: *What?*

TAYLOR: I just want to say . . . *(TAYLOR looks down, embarrassed.)* I'm sorry.

JAMIEL *(Putting hand to ear.)* What was that?

TAYLOR: *(Louder.)* I'm sorry. OK? I'm sorry.

JAMIE: Yeah?

TAYLOR: Yeah . . . It's just that . . . You know, it isn't always that easy being your sister/brother. *(TAYLOR looks at Jamie tensely.)* I mean, when you're around, everyone looks at *you.* When you talk, everyone stops and listens – and I just . . . disappear. I'm nothing but Jamie's little sister/brother. And then I just feel like I have to say something.

JAMIE: But why does it always have to be something *mean*? It could be like – I don't know. Anything but mean. Try it. Try saying something not mean.

TAYLOR: Yeah?

JAMIE: Yeah.

(TAYLOR fidgets and thinks for a few moments.)

TAYLOR: *(Embarrassed.)* I . . . I love you. *(JAMIE and TAYLOR look at each other for an extended moment.)* . . . That work?

JAMIE: *(Smiling.)* That works.

TAYLOR: *(Awkwardly.)* OK, well, I gotta go . . . do . . . something . . . now.

(TAYLOR starts to leave.)

JAMIE: *(Calling after Taylor.)* Hey.

TAYLOR: *(Stopping.)* Yeah?

JAMIE: Just thought you should know . . . I love you too.

TAYLOR: *(Looks at Jamie and smiles.)* Good to know.

JAMIE: *(Looks at Taylor and smiles.)*: Yeah. Good to know.

(TAYLOR exits. JAMIE looks after Taylor and continues smiling.)

– END SCENE –

POETRY

(Scene for three people.)

(NOTE: If ALEX is female, JESS is male. If ALEX is male, JESS is female. At start, ALEX is standing alone. After a moment, DREW enters and looks around uneasily, making sure no one else is there. DREW walks up to ALEX.)

DREW: You got . . . you know . . . *it?*

ALEX: *(Pulling out an envelope and handing it to DREW.)* Got it right here.

DREW: *(Taking envelope.)* Is it . . . good?

ALEX: It's really good.

DREW: Cuz I never really bought any – poetry before.

ALEX: Trust me, Jordan will love it.

DREW: Awesome.

ALEX: *(Holding out hand.)* That'll be five dollars.

DREW: Oh. Yeah. Got it right here.

(DREW hands over five dollars.)

ALEX: And don't forget. Poetry is only half of it. The other half is you.

DREW: *(Looking around to make sure no one is watching.)* Cool. Thanks. Gotta go.

(DREW exits. ALEX stands alone for a moment. Then JESS enters, looking around uneasily.)

JESS: *(Uncomfortably.)* Hey Alex.

ALEX: Hey Jess.

JESS: This is weird. I don't think we've ever actually talked before.

ALEX: Yeah, I don't think so.

JESS: My name is Jess.

ALEX: Yeah, I know. I'm Alex.

JESS: Right. Right. I heard you sell, like, customized poems?

ALEX: Yeah. I write them myself.

JESS: And they work?

ALEX: They're the best poems in town. You can ask anyone.

JESS: Yeah, I kinda heard that.

ALEX: So tell me what you need. *(ALEX starts listing types of poems.)* I can do secret crush, I never told you this before, Valentine's Day, I think we should break up. Anything you want. All five dollars each.

JESS: Wow, so I guess this one would be kind of "I never told you this before."

ALEX: Great. So what we do is, I'll ask you a couple of questions, take some mental notes, and then tomorrow you come back and I'll give you your poem. Sound good?

JESS: Um . . . I guess.

ALEX: Cool. So how long have you known this person?

JESS: Maybe a couple of years, but we're not like friends or anything.

ALEX: OK. And they go to school here?

JESS: Yes.

ALEX: So you see them every day.

JESS: Yeah, but we never talk.

ALEX: Hmm. And what do you want them to do when they get this poem?

JESS: I'm kind of hoping we could go to the winter dance.

ALEX: Wow. I've never actually been to the winter dance.

JESS: Yeah, me neither.

ALEX: I heard it's fun.

JESS: Everyone says so.

ALEX: So tell me something about this person.

JESS: He's/She's really smart. Kind of quiet, but super creative.

ALEX: OK.

JESS: Everyone knows who he/she is. But I think he's/she's actually kind of lonely.

ALEX: Huh.

JESS: He's/She's right about your height. And with your color hair. (*ALEX and JESS look at each other silently for a moment.*)

27

And with your same color eyes. And I think me and this person could have a lot of fun going to the winter dance together . . . and . . . stuff.

ALEX: . . . OK. And, um, just one more question . . . What's his/her name?

JESS: It's, um . . . It's . . . It's Alex.

ALEX: Yeah?

JESS: Yeah.

ALEX: I . . . I think I can write your poem right now. *(ALEX pulls out a small notebook and pen, quickly jots something down, tears out the page, folds it in half, and hands it to JESS.)* Here.

JESS: That's it?

ALEX: Yeah. But don't worry, I'm not going to charge you . . . Maybe you should read it right now to see if you like it.

JESS: Right now?

ALEX: Yeah, just to see . . . just to see if you like it.

JESS: OK. *(JESS unfolds paper and looks at it. Reading.)* Jess . . . Yes. *(JESS looks up at Alex.)*

ALEX: Do you like it?

JESS: Yeah. A lot.

ALEX: Do you want to go somewhere and talk?

JESS: Does it have to rhyme?

ALEX: Not even a little.

JESS: Cool.

ALEX: Cool.

(JESS and ALEX exit together.)

– END SCENE –

SUN

(Scene for two people.)

(At start, BAILEY and CHRIS are sunbathing, lying down on their backs, with their eyes closed. For the purposes of this scene, BAILEY and CHRIS could be actually lying down, but inclined so that the audience can see them, or they could be standing, but with body postures and movement as though lying down. Their eyes remain closed for most of the scene. Their conversation is slow and lazy.)

BAILEY: The sun is good today right?

CHRIS: So good. Not too hot.

> *(BAILEY and CHRIS sunbathe silently for a few moments.)*

BAILEY: Or too cold.

CHRIS: What?

BAILEY: The sun is not too cold.

CHRIS: No. Perfect.

BAILEY: Could you hand me the suntan lotion?

CHRIS: Is it to my right or my left? I don't feel like opening my eyes right now.

BAILEY: Mmmm - maybe left?

> *(CHRIS clumsily feels around with left hand for the lotion, but doesn't find it to the left.)*

CHRIS: I don't feel it.

BAILEY: Maybe right?

> *(CHRIS clumsily feels around with right hand for the lotion, but doesn't find it to the right.)*

CHRIS: Nothing.

BAILEY: Mmm – don't worry about it. *(BAILEY and CHRIS sunbathe silently for a moment.)* You ever think about skin cancer?

CHRIS: Not really.

BAILEY: Yeah, me neither.

CHRIS: What do you think we would do if we couldn't hang out and get tans?

BAILEY: I don't know. Nothing else is as much fun.

CHRIS: Or as easy.

BAILEY: And when you're finished, you look even better than when you started!

CHRIS: Totally.

> *(BAILEY suddenly stiffens, but still doesn't open eyes.)*

BAILEY: What was *that*?

CHRIS: What!?

BAILEY: I just felt something!

CHRIS: Oh wow, I feel it too.

BAILEY: I think it's a cloud going in front of the sun.

CHRIS: No!

BAILEY: Yes!

CHRIS: No!

BAILEY: Someone should look.

CHRIS: You do it.

BAILEY: No you do it.

CHRIS: OK. *(CHRIS cautiously opens one eye, then the other.)* It *is* a cloud!

BAILEY: No!

CHRIS: But it's really small. And there aren't any others.

BAILEY: Oh, phew!

(CHRIS closes both eyes again.)

CHRIS: Yeah, I think we're gonna be alright.

BAILEY: Hey, you didn't happen to see the suntan lotion when your eyes were open, did you?

CHRIS: Nah, I wasn't looking that way.

BAILEY: That's OK. One of us can look next cloud.

CHRIS: Yeah, next cloud.

> *(BAILEY and CHRIS smile and continue to sunbathe happily for another moment or two.)*

BAILEY and CHRIS: *(Simultaneously and contentedly.)*
  Mmmmm.

– END SCENE –

FAMILY

(Scene for two people.)

DALE: So I guess this is happening.

KELLY: I guess so.

DALE: There's just nothing right about this.

KELLY: Nothing.

DALE: I mean seriously. How could *your* dad be marrying *my* mom?

KELLY: It's kind of gross.

DALE: *(After a pause.)* I have to tell you something.

KELLY: What?

DALE: I never really liked you.

KELLY: Um, you think I don't know that? We've been going to school together since first grade. I never liked you either.

DALE: I know.

KELLY: Yeah.

DALE: Whose house do you think we're going to live in?

KELLY: Well, if it's my house, I'm not giving up my room.

DALE: Yeah? Well, if it's my house, I'm not giving up my room either.

KELLY: Fine.

DALE: Fine.

KELLY: So I guess we're gonna be sisters/brothers/brother and sister now.

DALE: I guess.

KELLY: That's weird.

DALE: Tell me about it. You think your friends will be nicer to me? After we're like . . . related?

KELLY: I guess if I told them to. You think your friends will be less weird?

DALE: I'm not sure if they know how.

>   *(DALE and KELLY look at each other a moment,*
>   *then break out laughing.)*

KELLY: You mean your friends *know* they're weird?

DALE: They know other people *think* they're weird. How could they not? And your friends don't know they're mean?

KELLY: Please. They practice being mean at home.

DALE: *(Amazed.)* Really?

KELLY: Like, a little bit.

>   *(THEY laugh.)*

DALE: I *knew* it! Tell you what, if you tell your friends to be nicer to me, I'll tell my friends to be nicer to you.

KELLY: But why would I want *your* friends to be . . .

DALE: *(Cutting KELLY off.)* Dude, we're related now. Just take the deal.

KELLY: Yeah? *(Thinks a moment.)* OK. Deal.

DALE: Family first.

KELLY: Family first.

(KELLY and DALE shake hands.)

DALE: Let's go, brother/sister.

KELLY: I'm right behind you.

(DALE and KELLY exit.)

– END SCENE –

DOING TIME

(Scene for two people.)

(ASH and VAL are in detention after school. At first, BOTH sit in chairs a few feet apart, with their hands between their knees, staring straight ahead. After a few moments ASH and VAL look over at each other, then look around to make sure the teacher is nowhere in sight.)

ASH: What are you in for?

VAL: Cursing. You?

ASH: Skipping gym.

VAL: Really?

ASH: Yeah.

VAL: But gym is so easy!

ASH: Not if you don't like gym.

VAL: I guess.

ASH: How much time are you serving?

VAL: I got three days' detention.

ASH: Really? For cursing?

VAL: At a teacher.

ASH: Whoa.

VAL: Yeah. You?

ASH: One day.

VAL: Cuz it's just gym.

ASH: Exactly. First time in?

VAL: I did some time upstate before I moved here. You know Porterville?

ASH: I heard it's really tough up there.

VAL: You have no idea. I did five days' detention there for doing practically nothing.

ASH: Cursing?

VAL: Spitting.

ASH: Dude. But five days?

VAL: Yeah. Repeat offender.

ASH: That's rough.

VAL: And upstate, the chairs they make you sit on are really small. And hard.

ASH: Wow. And I thought this was bad.

VAL: This place is like a resort compared to Porterville.

ASH: I hope my parents never move there.

VAL: I still have nightmares.

ASH: I had a cousin who did some time up there. Two days' detention for talking during a test. She's never been the same.

VAL: People who haven't been there can't understand.

ASH: *(Indicating a clock on the wall.)* Look. It's practically four o'clock. Detention is almost over.

VAL: Feels like it's been forever. No matter how many times I go through this, it never gets easier.

ASH: What are you doing after?

VAL: I thought I might get some soft serve ice cream.

ASH: I love soft serve ice cream.

VAL: You can come if you want.

ASH: Yeah?

VAL: Yeah. Once you've done time with someone, it's like a whole bonding thing.

ASH: I thought it might work like that.

(VAL suddenly looks offstage.)

VAL: There's the bell!

(VAL and ALEX stand up.)

ASH: Let's get out of here.

(THEY start to exit.)

VAL: So – you gonna keep skipping gym?

ASH: I don't know. It might not be worth all this. You gonna keep cursing?

VAL: I'm not sure I can help it.

ASH: I get that.

VAL: Cool. Meet you out front?

ASH: See you there.

(ALEX and VAL exit.)

– END SCENE –

MODERN ART

(Scene for two people.)

(The setting is a museum for modern art. After a moment, RILEY and SHANE enter.)

RILEY: This modern art class is really hard.

SHANE: Honestly, I don't get modern art at all.

RILEY: Like, why is every painting in this museum ugly?

SHANE: It doesn't matter. We still have to pick one and write about it.

RILEY: What about this one?

SHANE: Ugly.

RILEY: That one?

SHANE: Too weird.

RILEY: Yeah.

SHANE: Ehhh. Maybe this one?

RILEY: I don't know. What do you think it is?

SHANE: Like . . . a plant? Or maybe a person?

RILEY: Some sort of seashell?

SHANE : Could be.

RILEY: I feel like if we have to write about a painting for Mrs. Luddy, then we should at least know what the painting is.

41

SHANE: I guess. But what if we went sort of the other way?

RILEY: I have no idea what you're saying

SHANE: I mean, like, what if we pick a painting that we have no idea what it is, and then we say that that's what the artist was trying to do.

RILEY: You mean, like – this painting makes no sense, we have no idea what it is, and that's why it's such an amazing work of modern art?

SHANE: *(Getting excited.)* Exactly! But with bigger words.

RILEY: Oooh, hold on. I wrote down a bunch of big art words when Mrs. Luddy was talking before. *(RILEY pulls out a small notebook and opens it.)* Now say what you just said again.

SHANE: This painting makes no sense.

RILEY: Umm. Though we can never know for sure the artist's . . . *(RILEY looks down at notebook and searches for a word.)* . . . intentionality . . .

SHANE: Oh, nice word!

RILEY: Thank you. I wrote it down myself. *(Continuing.)* . . . The artist's intentionality, we can presumptively . . . *(Looking up from notebook.)* She used that word like three times . . . We can presumptively presume that the painting's . . . *(Frowning down at notebook.)* . . . apparent lack of . . . *(Glancing down at notebook.)* in-ter-pret-ability is intentional.

SHANE: That's really good!

RILEY: What did you say after that?

SHANE: *(Thinks a moment.)* Umm. We have no idea what this is.

RILEY: *(Looks down again at notebook.)* Oh my gosh, this is perfect!

SHANE: *(Eagerly.)* What?!? What?!?

RILEY: Though the painting is not literally a blank canvas, it serves as a blank canvas in the viewer's . . . brain.

SHANE: Whoa!

RILEY: Right? And I said "blank canvas" two times!

SHANE: We are totally gonna get an A!

RILEY: Maybe an A+!

SHANE: Do you think that's enough?

RILEY: Yeah, what else is there to say?

SHANE: Nothing.

RILEY: Exactly.

SHANE: OK, so that part's done. Now what should we bring in as our own modern art project?

RILEY: What about, like, a brick?

SHANE: Yeah! Or a crumpled up piece of paper.

RILEY: Or a crumpled up piece of paper sitting on top of a brick!

SHANE: Yes!

RILEY: And we'll call it "Brick."

SHANE: No! We'll call it "Thursday."

RILEY: That's genius.

SHANE: Oh man, I don't know what we were afraid of. Art is so easy.

RILEY: It's just like, stuff you make up.

SHANE: I bet Mrs. Luddy sure would be mad if she figured out that we haven't actually learned anything.

RILEY: So mad.

SHANE: So what should we do now?

RILEY: I dunno. You want to just look at the rest of the stuff? You know, just 'cuz?

SHANE: OK. I mean, we can look and see if there's anything better here than a brick with a crumpled up piece of paper on it.

RILEY: Ha! Not in a million years.

SHANE: Right?

(SHANE and RILEY exit.)

– END SCENE –

BUNKER

(Scene for three people.)

SAGE: I can't believe it.

CASSIDY: This is so weird.

LANE: There is nothing right about this.

SAGE: I mean, how could this happen?

CASSIDY: And why us?

LANE: OK, let's just think for a second. Are we absolutely, totally, like completely sure that we're the last three people on earth?

SAGE: Well, think about it. We knew for a fact when they were eighteen-thousand and seven people left, cuz there was still like communications and news reports and stuff.

LANE: Yeah.

CASSIDY: That's true.

SAGE: And then people just kept on disappearing until, you know . . . Last night when we went to bed there were only 16 people left and we were all right here in the bunker.

LANE: Yeah.

CASSIDY: Yeah.

SAGE: And when we woke up, they were all disappeared too. *(Pointing to self.)* One. *(Pointing to Lane.)* Two. *(Pointing to Cassidy.)* Three. *(Getting upset.)* I mean, you can count, right? We're the last three people on earth. Do the math.

45

LANE: Dude, relax. I'm not saying I think you're wrong. I'm just saying I *wish* you were wrong. OK? I don't *want* to be the practically last person on earth. That's all.

CASSIDY: Me neither. I hate this. Like, who's gonna make breakfast?

SAGE: *That's* what you're worried about?

CASSIDY: I mean – plus other stuff.

SAGE: Like . . . ?

CASSIDY: Like . . . lunch?

LANE: If you're so worried about it, why don't *you* just make the lunch. And then we'll all eat it.

CASSIDY: I'm not making lunch for all of you.

SAGE: Well, you wanted one of us to make lunch for you.

CASSIDY: That's different.

LANE: Is not.

CASSIDY: Is so.

SAGE: STOP! Just stop. What we need is some kind of way to make decisions. Like some kind of government.

CASSIDY : Fine. I volunteer to be King/Queen.

LANE: Yeah? Well I'm gonna to run for president.

SAGE: Well I'm gonna run against you. Ready? *(Raising hand.)* Who votes for me for president?

(LANE and CASSIDY don't raise their hands.)

LANE: Now who votes for *me* to be president? *(LANE raises hand. SAGE and CASSIDY don't raise their hands. LANE looks at Cassidy.)* You have to vote for *someone*.

CASSIDY: I'm not voting for anyone but me.

LANE: Fine.

SAGE: Fine.

CASSIDY: Fine.

SAGE: Well, if no one's going to be president, then I declare this whole part of the bunker to be my independent country. I'll make my own lunch.

LANE: Yeah? *(Pointing stage right.)* Well then that whole part of the bunker is *my* independent country. And I'm gonna make an even better lunch.

CASSIDY: Oh yeah? *(Pointing stage left.)* Well then *that* whole part of the bunker is *my* independent country. And my country is going to have the best lunches of all.

LANE: *(Getting up and starting to go to his/her part of the bunker.)* We'll see.

(LANE exits stage right.)

CASSIDY: *(Getting up and starting to go to his/her part of the bunker.)* Yeah, we'll see.

(CASSIDY exits stage left.)

SAGE: *(Looking left and right towards where Lane and Cassidy have just exited. To self, disgusted.)* Only three people left in the world, and I had to get stuck with those two.

– END SCENE –

BAND

(Scene for two people.)

RORY: So you really think we should try out for band?

JESS: Totally. It's, like, *making music!*

RORY: I know but . . .

JESS: *(Cutting RORY off.)* And we already know a ton of
people who are *in* band.

RORY: Yeah, but . . .

JESS: And people would be watching us and, like, maybe
getting jealous or whatever.

RORY: Yeah, but – like that part where people are watching
us . . . I mean . . .

JESS: What? Since when have you been shy?

RORY: I'm not being shy. It's just . . .

JESS: What? Just say it.

RORY: Jess, we don't play any instruments.

JESS: It'll be fine. Did you do what I told you? Did you sit
down last night and think about every possible instrument
you could maybe even play a little?

RORY: *(Hesitantly.)* Yeahhh.

JESS: And?

RORY: Well, I figure I could probably play the triangle. You know, it's just like one little . . . piece of metal. And it only plays one note and you just hit it with another piece of metal. I think I could do that.

JESS: That is excellent! I was thinking I could play the cymbals.
Like practically the same thing. It's just *two* pieces of metal, they play one note, and you just hit them with each other! We could be the, like . . . the metal things you hit with other metal things section! Those are like the best instruments in the entire band.

RORY: I know, but I was thinking about that and . . .

JESS: And what?

RORY: Isn't it the drummer who always plays those things?

JESS: But so what?

RORY: So if those are the best instruments, and the drummer always gets to hit them, why would he give that up?

JESS: I guess.

RORY: And on top of that, the drummer is Noah Peterson. He totally would not be OK with just giving that up.

JESS: Yeah. I guess.

RORY: So did you think about any other instruments we could play?

JESS: I mean, the harmonica is a great instrument.

RORY: I don't think they have harmonicas in band.

JESS: That's what makes it perfect! We would be the first. No competition!

49

RORY: But can you even play the harmonica?

JESS: Well, I mean, I *own* one.

RORY: But can you play it?

JESS: Not even a little.

RORY: Yeah.

JESS: Yeah.

RORY: So, listen. I did have this one other idea last night about something we could maybe play.

JESS: Yeah?

RORY: I mean, I don't know if it's a real instrument or not.

JESS: Like what?

RORY: I was thinking maybe we could play the kazoo.

JESS: Dude! That's perfect! I totally know how to play the kazoo!

RORY: Me too!

JESS: And no one else in band plays it.

RORY: And no one has to give anything up. *(RORY rolls eyes.)* Noah Peterson is unbelievable.

JESS: *(Disgusted.)* So selfish.

RORY: *(Pulling two kazoos out of pocket.)* And look. I even have two kazoos!

JESS: Awesome!

(JESS takes a kazoo.)

RORY: Should we rehearse?

JESS: Maybe once.

RORY: Ready? Try this.

> *(RORY starts to play "Off We Go into the Wild Blue Yonder." After a few moments – at the line "Climbing high into the sun" – JESS joins in and they BOTH play a few bars together – through the line "At 'em now, give 'em the gun." Any other up-tempo, marching band type song will also work.)*

JESS: Oh yeah, we got this.

RORY: Look out band, here we come!

JESS: Ready?

RORY: Ready.

> *(JESS and RORY start to play the song again, together. As they play, they BOTH start to march in a circle, then, as they approach the end of the first verse – the line "Nothing will stop the U.S. Air Force," they turn and, still playing, triumphantly march off the stage.)*

– THE END –

DELIVERY

(Scene for two people.)

(It's Christmas Eve. The reindeer DASHER and DANCER are pulling Santa's sleigh through the sky.)

DANCER: Hey Dasher! Dasher!

DASHER: What do you want Dancer? I'm working.

DANCER: Yeah, I know. We're all working here. Prancer is working. Blitzen is working. Comet is working. Rudolf is working.

DASHER: So?

DANCER: So how come we do all the work and Santa gets all the credit?

DASHER: Hunh.

DANCER: Right? I mean, Santa mostly just sits in the sleigh. We're the ones who have to pull the sleigh all around the world, *and* all the presents, *and* Santa. Who I might add, doesn't exactly get thinner every year.

DASHER: Yeah. Why *don't* we ever get any credit?

DANCER: It's not fair. And same thing with, like, horses who pull buggies. Why do they call it a buggy ride? Why don't they call it a horse pulling a buggy with you in it ride?

DASHER: Or babies.

DANCER: Babies?

DASHER: Yeah, it's a stork who delivers them right?

DANCER: Everyone knows that.

DASHER: But no one gets excited about the stork. It's always all about the baby.

DANCER: You know, I've got half a mind to go on strike.

DASHER: Yeah, maybe they'll appreciate us then.

DANCER: Let's see how fast these presents get delivered when Santa actually has to do the work.

DASHER: He breaks a sweat when he's sitting in a chair at the North Pole.

DANCER: Yeah, let's see him try and pull a sled at the equator.

DASHER: Still, he *is* a good boss.

DANCER: Yeah, like remember that time he threw us all a Christmas in July party?

DASHER: That was epic! Or that time he threw us a Christmas in August party?

DANCER: Or that Christmas in September party?

DASHER: And the one in October.

DANCER: And November.

DASHER: Yeah, Christmas is kind of his thing.

DANCER: True. And I guess it's not really his fault that people don't give us enough credit.

DASHER: It's not like he's out there shaking hands and telling everyone to ignore us.

DANCER: He basically never leaves the office. He's working 365 days a year.

DASHER: And all we really work is this one.

DANCER: Hey! What time is it?

DASHER: In what part of the world?

DANCER: Any part.

DASHER: I think we're like five minutes behind schedule.

DANCER: Can't have that.

DASHER: There are kids waiting.

DANCER: And Santa is depending on us.

DASHER: Faster?

DANCER: Faster.

DASHER: Let's go!

(DASHER and DANCER trot offstage together.)

– END SCENE –

ENCOUNTER

(Scene for two people.)

(At start, ALEX and KELLY are sitting several feet apart. KELLY is reading a book. THEY don't speak or interact for several moments.)

ALEX: *(Suddenly turning towards Kelly.)* Don't you hate it when strangers just start talking to you?

(KELLY looks up from book.)

KELLY: Umm . . . probably.

(KELLY goes back to reading.)

ALEX: The worst. So, what's your name?

(KELLY looks up from book.)

KELLY: Kelly.

(KELLY looks back down at book.)

ALEX: I'm Alex.

KELLY: *(Looking up from book.)* OK.

(KELLY closes book.)

ALEX: Like this kid last week just came up to me in the park and started talking about all his problems and whatever.

KELLY: *(Faking enthusiasm.)* Great!

ALEX: No, *not* great. He was telling me stuff I couldn't care less about.

KELLY: Right.

ALEX: What is wrong with people?

KELLY: Umm – lots of things?

ALEX: Yes! I am so glad we started talking. You want to hear something?

KELLY: Not really.

ALEX: You are so funny! How come we never met before?

KELLY: I don't talk to strangers.

ALEX: Yes! Yes! Yes! I can't believe how much we have in common!

KELLY: Like?

ALEX: We both hate talking to strangers. We live in the same town. Umm – all that stuff.

KELLY: Right.

ALEX: *(Enthusiastically.)* Right?

KELLY: . . . Right.

ALEX: So what are you doing now?

KELLY: Umm – I have a . . . dentist appointment in like . . . five . . . minutes.

ALEX: Ohhh – I *hate* dentist appointments.

KELLY: I think everyone does.

ALEX: Right? What are you doing after?

KELLY: Umm, a really important . . . ahh, piano lesson.

ALEX: Need company?

KELLY: For a piano lesson?

ALEX: Yeah!

KELLY: Definitely not. *(Standing up.)* OK, well, got to go to my . . . dentist . . . appointment.

ALEX: You come here a lot?

KELLY: Never. Will not be coming back.

ALEX: Oh. OK. Well, have a good life!

KELLY: Yeah, you too.

ALEX: Thanks! *(KELLY exits.)* Bye! *(Continuing to look after Kelley. Waving.)* Bye! *(ALEX sits dejectedly for a moment, then sees someone else offstage – in a different direction from where Kelly exited – and starts walking towards them.)* Hey! Hi! Don't you hate it when strangers just start talking to you? Like just now there was this kid here and he/she started telling me all about his/her *dental appointment.* Can you believe it? Wait up!

(ALEX exits.)

– END SCENE –

GO FISH

(Scene for two people.)

(At start, BRETT and JACKIE are fishing. BRETT is holding the fishing pole out over the water.)

JACKIE: What do you think?

BRETT: About what?

JACKIE: About this.

BRETT: What do you mean?

JACKIE: I mean – fishing – you think we're going to catch anything?

BRETT: *(Shrugging.)* Supposed to.

JACKIE: *Supposed* to? Who says?

BRETT: My dad. He goes fishing all the time.

JACKIE: Yeah?

BRETT: Yeah. He says that outside of a fishing pole and some bait, you only need three things to catch a fish. Patience, patience, and more patience.

JACKIE: He sounds like a real fun guy.

BRETT: I'm just saying, we got the pole. We got the bait. Let's just wait and see what happens.

JACKIE: It's been an hour.

(BRETT pulls out phone and checks the time.)

BRETT: It's been eleven minutes. Just wait a little. When it comes to stuff like fishing, my dad is never wrong.

JACKIE: Fine. *(JACKIE looks at the pole a moment. Looks at Brett moment. Looks at the pole again.)* But what if nothing happens?

BRETT: It will.

JACKIE: But what if it doesn't?

BRETT: It will.

JACKIE: But what if . . . *(JACKIE sees the fishing pole move and suddenly stops talking. Whispering excitedly.)* What was that?

BRETT: That's a fish.

JACKIE: *(Still talking quietly.)* Are you sure?

BRETT: What else could it possibly be? . . . And why are you whispering?

JACKIE: *(Still talking quietly.)* I don't want to scare it away.

BRETT: Dude, it's under water. It can't even hear us.

JACKIE: *(Glances at water, then speaks at normal volume.)* So what do we do now?

BRETT: We reel it in. But slowly. Like this. *(BRETT starts to slowly reel in the fish. After a moment.)* Wow, it's really fighting. I bet it's a flounder.

JACKIE: Why do you think it's a flounder?

BRETT: I don't know. It was the only fish I could think of.

JACKIE: Lemme try.

(BRETT hands JACKIE the fishing rod. JACKIE starts reeling in the fish.)

BRETT: But slowly.

JACKIE: *(Reeling the fish in more slowly and struggling with the rod.)* And it's really heavy. I bet it's a salmon!

BRETT: Because?

JACKIE: That's the only other fish I could think of.

BRETT: Let's reel it in together.

(BOTH hold onto the rod and try to reel the fish in. Continuing to struggle.)

JACKIE: I bet it's a shark!

BRETT: Or a whale!

JACKIE: Or a moose!

BRETT: What?!? *(Suddenly, the fishing line breaks. BRETT and JACKIE fall onto their backs.)* It got away!

JACKIE: *(Sitting up.)* Arghhh. It's not fair!

BRETT: *(Sitting up.)* It still counts! We still caught it! It's just that we caught it and then it got away.

JACKIE: Exactly. And it probably *was* a salmon.

BRETT: Or a shark.

JACKIEL Or a water moose.

BRETT: There's no such thing as a water moose.

JACKIE: *(Standing up.)* Whatever. We still caught it.

BRETT: *(Standing up.)* Totally.

JACKIE: We got any more of that bait?

BRETT: And more hooks too.

JACKIE: And we got all the patience in the world . . . Almost.

BRETT: Yeah. Look out little fish, we're coming to get you.
  (BRETT looks at Jackie.) Ready?

JACKIE: Ready.

– END SCENE –

DRAMA

(Scene for two females.)

(At start, NICKY is alone. BAILEY enters.)

BAILEY: Hey.

NICKY: Hey . . . You didn't bring your guitar?

BAILEY: I thought *you* were bringing a guitar.

NICKY: I don't own a guitar.

BAILEY: Ohh. Right. Right.

NICKY: It's OK. We can just, like, make up the songs in our heads and then figure out the guitar stuff later.

BAILEY: Totally.

NICKEY: Probably easier to do it that way anyhow.

BAILEY : So what should we write a musical about?

(NICKY and BAILEY think for several moments.)

NICKY: What about, like, this king and this queen in the middle-ages whose parents forced them to get married when they were like 12 or something and they don't like each other at all . . . So now they spend the entire show trying to kill each other. But in the end, they figure out that they really *are* in love. And then everybody's happy and they all sing.

BAILEY: Wow. I was more thinking maybe it should be, like, this girl in 8th grade or something who has this huge crush on this boy, but he doesn't even know it. And then . . . stuff happens and they all sing.

62

NICKY: Yeah, that's good too. Let's do that.

BAILEY: Cool.

NICKY: They are so going to love this show in drama club.

BAILEY: Totally.

NICKY: So what do you think the first song is?

BAILEY: I guess maybe the girl telling her best friend or, like, the bathroom mirror or something how much she really likes this boy.

NICKY: Yes! Genius!

BAILEY: What about . . . *(Sings tunelessly.)* I really, really like this boy.

NICKY : Ehhhh. How about –
        (Sings. To the tune of "Mary Had a Little Lamb.")
I so like this boy named Sage,
Boy named Sage,
Boy named Sage.

BAILEY: That's "Mary Had a Little Lamb."

NICKY: Darn it!

BAILEY: But why did you say Sage?

NICKY: What?

BAILEY: Why did you say you like this boy named Sage?

NICKY: No I didn't.

BAILEY: You just said it. In the song.

NICKY: That was the *character* saying that.

BAILEY: And after I just told you yesterday how much I like Sage.

NICKY: It's a musical. It's not real.

BAILEY: You can be honest. If you like Sage that's totally OK with me. Just tell me.

NICKY: Really?

BAILEY: Of course.

NICKY: I actually kind of do.

BAILEY: I knew it. I *knew* it! I guess that's why you wanted to write a musical about people who are always betraying each other.

NICKY: *What*?!? How am I betraying you? All I did was answer a question.

BAILEY: And make up a love song about my boyfriend.

NICKY: He's not your boyfriend. You've never even talked to him.

BAILEY: Whatever.

NICKY: And why are you being so crazy? It's not that important. Let's just write the show.

BAILEY: The *show*? This is not a show. This is my life. And you're ruining it.

NICKY: But . . .

BAILEY: I'm going home. I guess I see now why you didn't bring your guitar.

NICKY: What does that even mean?

BAILEY: As if you didn't know.

NICKY: *What?!?*

BAILEY: I'm out.

(BAILEY exits.)

NICKY: *(Yelling after Bailey.)* Guess I'll see you in drama. *(Louder.)* Get it? DRAMA? . . . *(Shaking head. To self.)* Some people. *(NICKY shrugs.)* Sheesh.

– END SCENE –

DRAMA

(Scene for two males.)

(At start, NICKY is alone. BAILEY enters.)

BAILEY: Hey.

NICKY: Hey . . . You didn't bring your guitar?

BAILEY: I thought *you* were bringing a guitar.

NICKY: I don't own a guitar.

BAILEY: Ohh. Right. Right.

NICKY: It's OK. We can just, like, make up the songs in our heads and then figure out the guitar stuff later.

BAILEY: Totally.

NICKEY: Probably easier to do it that way anyhow.

BAILEY : So what should we write a musical about?

(NICKY and BAILEY think for several moments.)

NICKY: What about, like, this king and this queen in the middle-ages whose parents forced them to get married when they were like 12 or something and they don't like each other at all . . . So now they spend the entire show trying to kill each other. But in the end, they figure out that they really *are* in love. And then everybody's happy and they all sing.

BAILEY: Wow. I was more thinking maybe it should be, like, this boy in 8th grade or something who has this huge crush on this girl, but she doesn't even know it. And then . . . stuff happens and they all sing.

66

NICKY: Yeah, that's good too. Let's do that.

BAILEY: Cool.

NICKY: They are so going to love this show in drama club.

BAILEY: Totally.

NICKY: So what do you think the first song is?

BAILEY: I guess maybe the boy telling his best friend or, like, the bathroom mirror or something how much he really likes this girl.

NICKY: Yes! Genius!

BAILEY: What about . . . . *(Sings tunelessly.)* I really, really like this girl.

NICKY : Ehhhh. How about –
  (Sings. To the tune of "Mary Had a Little Lamb.")
I so like this girl named Sage,
Girl named Sage,
Girl named Sage.

BAILEY: That's "Mary Had a Little Lamb."

NICKY: Darn it!

BAILEY: But why did you say Sage?

NICKY: What?

BAILEY: Why did you say you like this girl named Sage?

NICKY: No I didn't.

BAILEY: You just said it. In the song.

NICKY: That was the *character* saying that.

BAILEY: And after I just told you yesterday how much I like Sage.

NICKY: It's a musical. It's not real.

BAILEY: You can be honest. If you like Sage that's totally OK with me. Just tell me.

NICKY: Really?

BAILEY: Of course.

NICKY: I actually kind of do.

BAILEY: I knew it. I *knew* it! I guess that's why you wanted to write a musical about people who are always betraying each other.

NICKY: *What*?!? How am I betraying you? All I did was answer a question.

BAILEY: And make up a love song about my girlfriend.

NICKY: She's not your girlfriend. You've never even talked to her.

BAILEY: Whatever.

NICKY: And why are you being so crazy? It's not that important. Let's just write the show.

BAILEY: The *show*? This is not a show. This is my life. And you're ruining it.

NICKY: But . . .

BAILEY: I'm going home. I guess I see now why you didn't bring your guitar.

NICKY: What does that even mean?

BAILEY: As if you didn't know.

NICKY: *What*?!?

BAILEY: I'm out.

(BAILEY exits.)

NICKY: *(Yelling after Bailey.)* Guess I'll see you in drama. *(Louder.)* Get it? DRAMA? . . . *(Shaking head. To self.)* Some people. *(NICKY shrugs.)* Sheesh.

– END SCENE –

CAMPING

(Scene for two people.)

(WHITNEY and PARKER are outside, camping. At start, they're sitting on the ground in front of their tent.)

WHITNEY: Look at us, camping out like the cavemen!

PARKER: Living life in the wild.

WHITNEY: Nothing here but us and nature.

PARKER: So cool.

(WHITNEY and PARKER look around for a moment. Suddenly WHITNEY hears something.)

WHITNEY: Did you hear that?

PARKER: What?

(BOTH listen a moment. WHITNEY hears the sound again.)

WHITNEY: That!

PARKER: What do you think it is?

WHITNEY: Like either an owl or a vampire bat.

PARKER: Probably an owl.

WHITNEY: *(A little uncertainly.)* Yeah probably.

(BOTH look at their surroundings a moment.)

PARKER: Wow – it gets dark out here really fast.

WHITNEY: I bet it's not this dark inside.

PARKER: Yeah, with like, electricity and stuff.

WHITNEY: Yeah, with like, electricity for soft, civilized people.

PARKER: Not for cavemen.

WHITNEY: Or people who live in nature like us.

PARKER: *(Suddenly hearing something.)* Whoa - did you hear that?

WHITNEY: Definitely a vampire bat.

PARKER: It totally was.

> *(WHITNEY and PARKER look around uneasily for a few moments.)*

WHITNEY: Do you think maybe camping out here wasn't the best idea?

PARKER: I mean, it *seemed* like a good idea. You know, inside.

WHITNEY: It's probably fine.

PARKER: Yeah – why wouldn't it be? *(WHITNEY and PARKER look around uneasily for another moment.)* Think there are any bears out here?

WHITNEY: No. I mean, probably no. Almost definitely probably no.

PARKER: We should start a fire.

WHITNEY: *(Excitedly.)* That would be amazing!

(WHITNEY and PARKER look at each other a moment.)

PARKER: Did you bring any matches?

WHITNEY: No.

PARKER: Me neither.

WHITNEY: Hunh.

PARKER: Want to tell ghost stories?

WHITNEY: No! Definitely not.

PARKER: It's really weird out here, away from civilization.

WHITNEY: Right? I have no idea how the cavemen did it.

PARKER: I don't know if I can make it through the whole night.

WHITNEY: Me neither.

PARKER: I bet back home they're all watching TV right now. Like all soft and civilized.

(WHITNEY squints into the distance.)

WHITNEY: I can kind of see them through the window. They're definitely watching TV.

PARKER: Figures. They hardly even *know* what nature is.

WHITNEY: Ridiculous.

PARKER: Still . . . I bet they have popcorn.

(WHITNEY squints towards the house.)

WHITNEY: They totally do. I can *see* it.

PARKER: You know, a little popcorn wouldn't be the worst thing in the world.

WHITNEY: Yeah. And if we want, we can always camp in the backyard tomorrow night.

PARKER: Or the night after that.

WHITNEY: Yeah, probably the night after that.

PARKER: Definitely.

WHITNEY: *(Standing up.)* Should we go?

PARKER: *(Standing up.)* Let's go.

WHITNEY: *(Starting to walk towards the house. Yelling.)* Hey Mom, we're home!

PARKER: *(Starting to walk towards the house behind Whitney. Yelling.)* Save us some popcorn!

WHITNEY: *(Looking back at Parker.)* Hurry up!

(WHITNEY and PARKER exit.)

– END SCENE –

CHAT

(Scene for two people.)

> *(PAT and AVERY are hanging out. Throughout, AVERY is holding – and constantly checking – a cellphone.)*

PAT: What do you want to do later?

AVERY: Hold on.

> *(PAT waits patiently for a few moments while AVERY looks at phone and writes a text.)*

PAT: So?

AVERY: *(Looking up from phone.)* So – what?

PAT: What do you want to do later?

AVERY: Ummmm . . . *(AVERY suddenly gets distracted by a text alert and looks at phone.)* Oh! Text! *(Frowns at phone for a moment. To Pat.)* It's Jamie again. Can you believe those guys?

PAT: Probably. So, do you wanna go hang out at the mall?

AVERY: *(Looking at phone and texting.)* Um, when?

PAT: *(Annoyed.)* Later. Today.

AVERY: *(Still looking at phone.)* Ha! Do you want to hear what Morgan just said?

PAT: Not really.

AVERY: This is hilarious.

PAT: So, do you want to?

AVERY: Hold on a sec. *(AVERY texts for a moment.)* Ha! *(Looking up from phone.)* Do I want to do what?

PAT: *(Extremely annoyed.)* Do. You. Want. To. Go. To. The. Mall.

AVERY: Today?

PAT: YES. Later today.

AVERY: Lemme check the weather.

PAT: It's a mall. We'll be inside. It will be warm and not sunny.

AVERY: *(Fiddling with phone.)* Well, it's always good to check.

PAT: *(Waits impatiently a few moments.)* Sooo . . .

AVERY: So now Jamie is saying . . .

PAT: *(Angrily.)* I don't care what Jamie is saying!

AVERY: Well you don't have to be rude about it!

PAT: I'm asking you a simple question. Do you want to go to the mall later?

AVERY: Well why didn't you just say so? I mean . . . *(AVERY is distracted by another text alert.)* Oh – hold on. *(Avery starts texting.)* Ha! Too funny.

PAT: You know what? Forget it.

(PAT starts to walk away.)

AVERY: *(Looking up from phone.)* Where are you going? You can't just walk away like that in the middle of a

(Cont.)

conversation. *(PAT exits. AVERY looks after Pat for a moment. To self.)* Some people are so rude. *(AVERY gets distracted by a text alert and looks at phone.)* Ha! Oh no they didn't! Morgan is gonna love this! *(AVERY starts texting again.)*

– END SCENE –

POPULAR

(Scene for two people.)

KENDAL: How did we get here?

ROYCE: Right?

KENDAL: I mean, we're fun.

ROYCE: So fun.

KENDAL: And interesting.

ROYCE: *Really* interesting.

KENDAL: Smart.

ROYCE : Probably smarter than average.

KENDAL: So why aren't we, you know, popular?

ROYCE: Makes no sense.

KENDAL: I mean, you're so cool that even if other people *wanted* to hang out with me, it would still be you I'd hang out with.

ROYCE: Same here!

KENDAL: So why doesn't anyone else want to hang out with us? What are we doing wrong?

ROYCE: Like, maybe our clothes?

KENDAL: Maybe. *(Looking at Royce's jacket.)* Like people are always saying how ridiculous that jacket looks.

ROYCE: I know. (*Looking at KENDAL's hat.*) And they say the same thing about that hat.

KENDAL: They do?

ROYCE: Sorry. So what else?

KENDAL: What about if we joined a sports team?

ROYCE: Yes!

KENDAL: Or came to school every day with, like, a pet iguana or something.

ROYCE: *So* cool.

KENDAL: Right?

ROYCE: I have to tell you though, I'm a little bit afraid of iguanas.

KENDAL: Me too.

ROYCE: Hmm. What if we threw a party?

> (*KENDAL and ROYCE look at each other for an extended moment.*)

KENDAL and ROYCE: (*Simultaneously.*) No.

KENDAL: (*Summing up.*) OK so, new clothes, yes. Pet iguana, no. Join sports team, yes. Throw party, no. You think that's enough?

ROYCE: I doubt it.

KENDAL: So *think*. What else is popular?

ROYCE: Mallomars are popular.

KENDAL: That's true . . . You got any?

ROYCE: In the kitchen.

KENDAL: You know what? We can figure out this whole popularity thing tomorrow.

ROYCE: And eat Mallomars today.

> *(KENDAL and ROYCE start to head towards the kitchen.)*

KENDAL: This is why we're actually so much fun to hang out with.

ROYCE: Cuz we got Mallomars?

KENDAL: And no iguanas.

ROYCE: Yup. Popularity here we come!

> *(ROYCE and KENDAL exit.)*

– END SCENE –

GOSSIP

(Scene for three people.)

DYLAN: Did you hear about Caitlin?

TERRY: *(Excitedly.)* No – tell me!

DYLAN: I heard that she pretended to trip in front of Jason outside of art class so that he would catch her. And then he didn't even notice, and she fell right on her face!

TERRY: Oh wow.

DYLAN: Right?

TERRY: 'Cuz I heard that it was *Kerry* who pretended to trip in front of *Jared*, and that he *caught* her and now they're meeting at the mall after school.

DYLAN: No!

TERRY: Yes!

DYLAN: Well get *this*. Evan said he was sitting right behind Peter Nolan's mom at soccer practice. And he heard Peter's mom say that if Peter doesn't raise his grades like immediately, she's gonna make him quit the soccer team!

TERRY: But Peter's the captain!

DYLAN: I know! But then Evan also said that he wasn't completely sure if it was Peter's mom or not, and they might have been talking about someone else.

TERRY: But even so!

DYLAN: Right? Well, *listen to this . . .*

(JJ enters and waves hi to Terry.)

TERRY: *(To JJ.)* Oh hey.

JJ: *(To Terry.)* Hey.

DYLAN: *(To Terry.)*: Who's this?

TERRY: Oh, this is my new friend I just met from history class. She's/He's cool.

DYLAN: *(To JJ.)* Hey.

JJ: *(To Dylan.)* Hey. *(To both.)* So what are you guys doing?

DYLAN: I was just gonna tell about this kid JJ I heard about, who supposedly swallowed a live goldfish in science class on a bet.

TERRY: *What?*

(TERRY and JJ look at each other for a moment.)

DYLAN: *(Looking back and forth at Terry and JJ.)* What?

JJ: *(Looks at Terry and Dylan for an extended moment.)* I'm JJ.

DYLAN: Oh.

TERRY: *(To Dylan.)*: Yeah.

DYLAN: *(To JJ.)* Really?

JJ: Yeah.

DYLAN: *(To JJ, uncertainly.)* So . . . is it true?

(JJ looks at Dylan and Terry expressionlessly for a moment, then breaks into a smile.)

JJ: Totally!

TERRY: That's awesome!

DYLAN: You know, sometimes it's so hard to tell around here what's true and what's not.

JJ: *(Happily.)* Well that story is totally true. Is anyone else heading to the cafeteria?

TERRY: I am.

DYLAN: I am.

(ALL THREE start to exit.)

JJ: So did you guys hear that some kid got sent home this morning either for skipping English too many times or for getting into a fight?

TERRY: I heard it was a sore throat.

DYLAN: I heard he had to help his grandmother with something.

JJ: No!

TERRY: Wow.

DYLAN: There is just so much going on around here, I don't know how anyone keeps track.

JJ: Right?

(ALL THREE exit.)

– END SCENE –

TIME

(Scene for two people.)

VAL: You ever wish you could go back in time?

DREW: You mean like to the dinosaurs?

VAL: No, more like inside your own life.

DREW: Huh.

VAL: Like if I could wake up one morning and say, today I'm gonna go back to the first day I met Drew.

DREW: Hah. We were at Mary Ann Cabrini's birthday party. Remember?

VAL: Yes! Second grade.

DREW : And you were like standing in the corner crying 'cuz someone spilled root beer on your shirt.

VAL: I wasn't crying.

DREW: You were crying.

VAL: Well maybe a little.

DREW: And I had just moved here like a week before. I don't even know how I got invited. But all I wanted was for someone to be my friend. And there you were, like, dripping with root beer.

VAL: And you walked over all tough and you said *(Speaking in a tough voice.)*, "Don't worry about it. Everyone spills root beer sometimes." And you spilled a whole glass all over yourself!

DREW: I had no idea how to start a conversation.

VAL: Guess you figured that one out.

DREW: Mrs. Cabrini called your mom like instantly and made her take us both back to your house.

VAL: *(Laughing.)* Total scandal.

DREW : Remember what we did?

VAL: Yeah. We tried to give the cat a bath!

DREW: Timmy the cat. Do you think that's why he ran away?

VAL: No. That was like a year later.

DREW: I guess that's true.

VAL: But maybe if I could, one day I'd go back inside my own life and spend another afternoon with Timmy. He was a good cat.

DREW: *(Hesitantly.)* Think one day in the future you'll ever want to go back to today?

VAL: You mean to right now?

DREW: More or less.

VAL: Probably more like to yesterday or last week or last month.

DREW: . . . Yeah . . . Probably more like then.

> *(DREW and VAL look at each other.)*

VAL: I'm gonna miss you.

DREW: I can't believe I have to move to Ohio. Hey – you're

(Cont.)
not gonna start crying again are you, like that first day?

VAL: I wasn't crying then. *(VAL looks at Drew.)* Or maybe a little.

DREW: . . . I'm gonna miss you too.

VAL: . . . But hey – I hear they got cellphones in Ohio.

DREW: *(Trying to smile.)* Yeah, FaceTime too.

VAL & DREW: *(Simultaneously.)* Texting. *(VAL and DREW look at each other, then speak simultaneously again.)* Jinx!

(BOTH laugh.)

DREW: *(After a moment.)* Well, I guess my mom is waiting.

VAL: I know.

DREW: Out in the car.

VAL: Yeah.

DREW: *(Not wanting to leave. Sadly.)* Bye Val.

VAL: *(Sadly.)* Bye Drew.

(VAL and DREW look at each other a moment. DREW exits.)

VAL: *(Looking where Val exited. Sadly.)* Bye.

– END SCENE –

AFTERNOON

(Scene for two people.)

(JINGLES and BOO BOO are house cats. At start, BOTH are doing typical cat things – grooming themselves, using one paw to scratch rapidly behind an ear, etc. After several moments of cat behavior, JINGLES speaks.)

JINGLES: You think there's any cat food left in the bowl?

BOO BOO: Nah. I was in the kitchen a while ago and it was empty.

JINGLES: Thought so . . . What time is Jimmy getting back?

BOO BOO: I don't know. I'm a cat. I can't tell time.

JINGLES: Oh right. Yeah. Me neither.

BOO BOO: There's water.

JINGLES: What?

BOO BOO: There's water in the other bowl.

JINGLES: I'd rather just drink out of the toilet. It's closer.

BOO BOO: Yeah. And Jimmy flushes a fresh bowl, like, all the time.

JINGLES: Yeah.

BOO BOO: So what do you want to do this afternoon?

JINGLES: I don't know. I was thinking of maybe taking a nap.

86

BOO BOO: Oooh. That's a really good idea.

JINGLES: Maybe Jimmy will get here before we wake up.

BOO BOO: Definitely. Time flies when you're taking a nap.

JINGLES: *(Suddenly sitting straight up and getting excited.)* Whoa! Did you see that?

BOO BOO: What?

JINGLES: The second you said "flies," a fly just landed on the table! Here it comes!

> *(BOTH excitedly try to swat at the fly, without quite catching it.)*

BOO BOO: Got you!

JINGLES: Got you!

BOO BOO: Got you!

JINGLES: Wow, this one's fast!

BOO BOO: Aw – there it goes out the window.

JINGLES: Next time.

BOO BOO: Definitely.

> *(JINGLES yawns, then BOO BOO yawns.)*

JINGLES: Look. The sun is just beginning to hit the floor over there.

BOO BOO: That looks like the perfect place for a nap.

JINGLES: If we just wait here, the sunny spot will get to us eventually.

BOO BOO: I guess that's true.

JINGLES: Same as yesterday.

BOO BOO: Oh yeah.
> *(Still sitting up, BOTH very slowly start to close their eyes. After a moment, BOO BOO opens eyes and speaks.*
Think there's any food left in the bowl?

JINGLES: Nah. I was in the kitchen a while ago and it was empty.

BOO BOO: Oh. Right.

> *(BOTH lie down and slowly close their eyes.)*

JINGLES: *(Half asleep.)* I guess we should just wait until the sunny spot gets here.

> *(JINGLES rolls over on back, hands and knees pointing up.)*

BOO BOO: *(Half asleep.)* And Jimmy gets here.

> *(BOO BOO curls up on side, head resting on arm.)*

JINGLES: I'm gonna dream about dry food.

BOO BOO: I'm gonna dream about wet food.

BOTH: *(Simultaneously. Almost asleep.)* Fooood.

> *(BOTH fall asleep.)*

– END SCENE –

OUTER SPACES

(Scene for two people.)

(At start, RORY and CASEY are sitting on a sofa, playing a video game. Each holds a real or imaginary controller. At start, they are making combat sounds of swords and laser guns.)

RORY: Clang – clang, clang!

CASEY: Pew – pew, pew, pew!

RORY: I'm taking out my bumblebee bazooka and shooting killer bees at you! Shump! Shump!

CASEY: I'm grabbing my billygoat billy club and batting them back at you! Whack! Whack! Whack!

ROREY: I'm jumping behind an ant hill and shooting muskrat missiles.

CASEY: Ha! They're no match for my fleet of fighting falcons! Down they go! Plop! Plop, plop!

RORY: All right then, you'll never escape this! I'm throwing my buffalo bomb! BOOM! I got you!

CASEY: Too slow! I'm already deploying my turtle shell shield!

RORY: Nuh-unh. I just took your last life. You're gone!

CASEY: Nuh-unh. I was too fast for you.

ROREY: It says right on the screen, you have no more lives left.

CASEY: Doesn't matter. Sometimes the, like, software in these things is broken. That's a total mistake.

RORY: You can't just decide that the score is wrong because you feel like it.

CASEY: You know what? I don't want to play this anymore.

RORY: Yeah, me neither. We've already been playing for like four hours.

CASEY: So what should we play? What other games do you have?

(BOTH sit in silence for a moment.)

ROREYL *(Uneasily.)* Do you want to try playing . . . like . . . outside?

CASEY: You mean . . . outside the living room?

RORY: Not exactly.

CASEY: You mean outside . . . the *house*?

RORY: Yeah, like in the backyard.

CASEY: Outside the house in the backyard?

ROREY: Yeah, like outside outside.

CASEY: But we've never done that. All we've ever done is play video games.

RORY: I know.

CASEY: Do people actually play outside anymore? Like what would we even do out there?

(BOTH think in silence for a moment.)
RORY: I remember when I was little . . .

CASEY: Yeah?

RORY: Like before I ever played a video game . . .

CASEY: Yeah?

RORY: We used to . . . I mean, outside we used to . . .

CASEY: What?

ROREY: Are you *ready*?

CASEY : Just say it!

RORY: *(Quickly.)* Set! Go! *(Tagging Casey.)* Tag! You're it!

> *(RORY runs out of the room. CASEY calls after Rory.)*

CASEY: But I didn't even . . . *(To self.)* Wait, I remember this one! *(CASEY stands up. Calls after RORY.)* Wait up! You'll never win! *(To self. Amazed.)* Outside the house . . . in the backyard! Whoa!

> *(CASEY runs off after RORY.)*

– END SCENE –

PANIC

(Scene for two people.)

> *(At start, CHRIS and NICKY are walking to a friend's house. CHRIS lags behind Nicky.)*

NICKY: Hurry *up*! This is gonna be epic. It's gonna to be the party of the year!

CHRIS: *(Uncertainly.)* Yeah.

NICKY: And I think Aaaalex will be there.

CHRIS: *(Still uncertainly.)* I know.

NICKY: It's gonna be totally awesome!

CHRIS: *(Without real enthusiasm.)* Yeah. Definitely.

NICKY: You don't seem very excited.

CHRIS : *(Breathing quickly.)* No, I . . . I totally am.

NICKY: What is *up* with you today?

CHRIS: *(Breathing quickly.)* I . . .

NICKY: What?

> *(CHRIS continues to breathe quickly for the next several lines.)*

CHRIS: I . . .

NICKY: What?

CHRIS: I . . .

NICKY: *What?*

CHRIS: I think I'm having a panic attack.

NICKY: What do you mean?

CHRIS: I need to sit down.

NICKY: Now?

CHRIS: *(Sitting down.)* Right now.

NICKY: What is going on?

CHRIS: I can't . . .

NICKY: I mean, are you afraid of Alex?

CHRIS: It's not that specific.

NICKY: Are you afraid of the party?

CHRIS: Like – yes, but no. *(Taking a few deep breaths.)* Panic attacks don't work like that.

NICKY: *(Sitting down next to Chris.)* So how do they work?

CHRIS: It's, like, not one thing. It's like all of a sudden *everything* is too much. I . . . I can't deal.

NICKY: Like *everything*?

CHRIS: *(Frantically.)* Yes! Like everything! Everything in the world is too much.

NICKY: Like scary much.

CHRIS: Like scary much.

NICKY: So – does just sitting here with me scare you?

CHRIS: *(Thinking a moment.)* No. Not really. *(Beginning to breathe more normally.)* It's like everything . . . out there. Everything I can't see right now. Like the party. Like whatever might happen tomorrow. Or the next day. Like – everything.

NICKY: But what if you had something with you that didn't scare you?

CHRIS: What do you mean?

NICKY: Like me. What if I'm there with you at the party? I'm gonna be there too.

CHRIS: I mean . . .

NICKY: And tomorrow. I'll be around. And if I'm not, you can call me. I mean, you're not scared *all* the time, right?

CHRIS: No! It doesn't even happen every day. Sometimes not even for like a week.

NICKY: So?

CHRIS: And then I could call you? Or we could hang out or something?

NICKY: Yeah.

CHRIS: That would be good. That would be really good.

NICKY: So what do you think?

CHRIS: About what?

NICKY: Are you ready to go to the party?

CHRIS: Huh. Yeah – I think I am.

NICKY: *(Standing up. Enthusiastically.)* Then let's do this!

CHRIS: *(Standing up. Almost as enthusiastically.)* Yeah. Let's do this!

(CHRIS and NICKY start walking.)

NICKY: And you know – Aaaalex will be there.

CHRIS: *(Looking at Nicky.)* Don't worry. I got this.

NICKY: *(Smiling at Chris.)* Yeah. You got this.

(CHRIS and NICKY exit, smiling.)

– THE END –

LEMONS

(Scene for two people.)

(AUBREY and JACKIE have just gotten their frisbee stuck in a tree. At start, BOTH enter, looking up into the tree where the frisbee is. JACKIE holds a pantomime soccer ball.)

AUBREY: Do you see it?

JACKIE: *(Circling the tree.)* I know it's up there.

AUBREY: It's got to be.

JACKIE: I told you not to throw the frisbee so high.

AUBREY: It's no fun if you don't.

JACKIE: *(Annoyed.)* Fine.

AUBREY : I see it!

JACKIE: Where?

AUBREY: *(Pointing.)* There. In that big branch.

JACKIE: Whoa. I'm not climbing that.

AUBREY: Well, I'm not climbing it.

JACKIE: You're the one who threw the frisbee.

(AUBREY looks up at the tree for a moment.)

AUBREY: I have a better idea.

JACKIE: What?

AUBREY: Let's just throw the soccer ball at it.

JACKIE: OK, me first.

> *(JACKIE takes the soccer ball, throws it at the frisbee and misses. In unison, BOTH watch the ball go up, then come down.)*

AUBREY: Not even close. My turn.

> *(AUBREY retrieves the soccer ball, throws it at the frisbee and misses. In unison, BOTH watch the ball go up, then continue to stare up into the tree for a moment.)*

JACKIE: Oh my gosh. What did you do?

AUBREY: I didn't do anything.

JACKIE: Now the soccer ball is stuck in the tree.

AUBREY: Whatever. My dad always says, when life hands you lemons, make lemonade.

> *(JACKIE stares at Aubrey.)*

JACKIE: What does lemonade have to do with you losing a frisbee *and* a soccer ball? That belong to me.

AUBREY: It just seemed like the right time to say it. *(AUBREY looks up at tree for a moment.)* OK, here's what we do. You tell *your* mom that I lost the frisbee and soccer ball, and I'll tell *my* mom that you lost them.

JACKIE: You *did* lose the frisbee and soccer ball.

AUBREY: Just sayin'.

JACKIE: *(Annoyed.)* Fine.

AUBREY: Anyhow, I got another soccer ball at my house. And probably a frisbee. That's what my dad would call lemonade.

JACKIE: We already *had* the soccer ball and frisbee lemonade. Til you lost them.

AUBREY: Just go with it. Then we can all move on.

JACKIE: Fine. Lemonade, here we come!

(JACKIE and AUBREY exit.)

– END SCENE –

HEALTHY

(Scene for two people.)

(At start, JACKIE and QUINN are standing at the kitchen counter with a carton of milk, a large measuring cup, two glasses, and a number of bottles and cans in front of them. These items should all be indicated by pantomime when they are used.)

QUINN: Are you sure this will work?

JACKIE: I'm telling you, this is a million dollar idea. Maybe even a billion.

QUINN : I sure could use a billion dollars.

JACKIE : Yeah, me too.

QUINN: So what is all this?

JACKIE : OK. Every time my dad goes to one of those smoothie places and gets like a *healthy* smoothie, he always makes this face and says, "Ugh - Jackie, the worse it tastes, the healthier it is for you."

QUINN: Hunh.

JACKIE: And we're talking some nasty stuff. Like kale and plant seeds and goat milk . . .

QUINN: Ugh! From real goats?

JACKIE: Yeah. And like beets and spinach and ground up beetles and I don't know what.

QUINN: That is so disgusting.

JACKIE: Yeah, but my dad keeps going back. And so do all these other people.

QUINN: Hunh.

JACKIE: And they're charging like $12 for a big paper cup of this stuff.

QUINN : Wow.

JACKIE : Exactly. So I started thinking, what if we could invent something even more disgusting?

QUINN: It would be like the healthiest drink in the world!

JACKIE: And we could charge like . . . *thirteen* dollars for a cup!

QUINN: Whoa.

> *(JACKIE indicates all the bottles and cans and objects on the counter.)*

JACKIE: So this is everything from the spice cabinet, stuff from the bathroom, stuff from all the rest of the house. Things I picked up off the ground in the park. Just about every disgusting thing I could find or think of. But only if it tasted really bad and was probably healthy.

QUINN: We are gonna be so rich!

JACKIE: Maybe even make a *trillion* dollars!

QUINN: At least!

JACKIE: *(Picking up a carton of milk and opening it.)* OK, so let's just start with this milk.

> *(JACKIE holds the milk under QUINN's nose.)*

QUINN: *(Pulling back, disgusted.)* Whoa.

JACKIE: Yeah. It's like three weeks old.

QUINN: Perfect!

> *(JACKIE pours the milk into the big measuring cup.)*

JACKIE: But that's not enough. A really healthy smoothie has like . . . ingredients.

QUINN: *(Picking up small bottle.)* I'm right behind you. Let's put in this . . . *(Looking at the small bottle's label.)* Tabasco sauce.

JACKIE: Cool.

> *(QUINN dumps some Tabasco sauce into the measuring cup.)*

QUINN: *(Picking up small bottle.)* And this . . . *(Looking at label.)* Garlic powder.

> *(QUINN pours garlic powder into the measuring cup.)*

JACKIE: How about these weeds I got at the park?

QUINN: Do it! *(JACKIE drops weeds in the measuring cup. QUINN picks up another bottle.)* Vinegar?

JACKIE: Definitely. And let's dump in this mouthwash too!

> *(QUINN and JACKIE pour some of their bottles into the measuring cup. QUINN picks up another small spice bottle.)*

QUINN: What's . . . *(Squinting at label.)* . . . tur . . . mer . . . ic?

JACKIE: Who knows. Throw it in. (*QUINN pours some turmeric into the measuring cup as JACKIE picks up a salt shaker.*) Salt?

QUINN: (*Giggling.*) And pepper!

> (*QUINN and JACKIE shake salt and pepper into the measuring cup.*)

JACKIE: Anything else?

QUINN: (*Picking up a container of liquid soap.*) Maybe just a little bit of soap. I mean, what's healthier than soap, right?

JACKIE: Totally.

QUINN: OK, now I'll stir it up. (*JACKIE picks up a spoon and stirs the smoothie very rapidly and aggressively, then pours a some into a glass. Holding glass out to Jackie.*) Want to taste it?

JACKIE: No – you taste it.

QUINN: OK, we'll both taste it . . . (*QUINN takes a second glass, fills it with smoothie, hands it to JACKIE, and picks up first glass.*) Ready? . . . Go! (*BOTH drink some of the smoothie, then immediately make horrified, disgusted faces.*) Ugh.

JACKIE: Oh my gosh.

QUINN: Ugh!

JACKIE: Oh my gosh!

QUINN: *Ugh!*

JACKIE: *Oh. My. Gosh!*

QUINN: That tastes really, really . . . healthy.

JACKIE: I think I'm gonna be sick.

QUINN: Wow. If you do, we could also sell this as a weight loss drink!

JACKIE: Yes! What comes after a trillion?

QUINN: Like, a gazillion.

JACKIE: We are going to make a gazillion dollars off of this!

QUINN: At least!

JACKIE: *(Holding up glassful of the smoothie.)* Here's to us.

QUINN: *(Holding up glassful of the smoothie.)* To us.

> *(JACKIE and QUINN look at the glasses in their hands, then look at each other, then look back at the glasses.)*

JACKIE: *(Putting glass down on the counter without drinking any.)* We should probably save this.

QUINN: Yeah, it's worth like a gazillion dollars. *(Putting glass down on the counter without drinking any.)* Wanna go watch TV?

JACKIE Yeah. You got any soda?

QUINN: We got a ton in the fridge.

JACKIE: Sounds healthy to me. Let's go.

> *(JACKIE and QUINN exit.)*

– END SCENE –

THE TRUE STORY

(Scene for four people.)

(Throughout the scene, everyone is facing forward. BLAIR and WHITNEY are the farthest apart, with REED and JORDAN in the space between them. Except where noted, ALL speak towards the audience, not to each other.)

BLAIR: My name is Blair, and this is the true story of what happened with me and my pencil.

WHITNEY: My name is Whitney, and this is the *actually* true story of what happened with that pencil.

REED: My name is Reed, and all I know is what I saw from across the room.

JORDAN: And my name is Jordan. I didn't *see* anything. *(Cupping ear with hand in a listening gesture.)* But I was in the very next room, where they have this air vent that lets you hear everything that goes on in the room where Blair and Whitney were. *(Lowers hand.)*

BLAIR: We were taking this English test in Mrs. Tyler's class.

WHITNEY: We were in homeroom with Mr. Kennedy and everyone was just sitting around joking.

REED: It was all a long time ago, but I think we were in Social Studies, talking about the American Revolution or something.

JORDAN: Mr. Kennedy had just sent me next door to the supply room to get a box of chalk, when all of a sudden, through the vent, I heard Blair and Whitney start arguing.

104

BLAIR: So we're in the middle of this English test when out of nowhere my pencil point breaks. *(Momentarily glancing at Whitney, then back towards the audience.)* Whitney always brings a second pencil for tests, and it was sitting right there on her/his desk. So I said, "Hey, can I borrow your other pencil."

WHITNEY: *(Momentarily glancing at Blair, then back towards the audience.)* I don't really understand *what* happened. We're just sitting around homeroom, joking, and all of a sudden Blair says to me, "That's my pencil."

REED: I look up, and I can see from across the room that Blair and Whitney are arguing, but I don't know what it's about.

JORDAN: *(Cupping ear with hand in a listening gesture, and continuing to cup ear for most of the rest of the scene.)* First, through the vent, I hear Blair say something about a pencil, and then I hear Whitney – like really angry – say, "You can't just take that."

BLAIR: Like all I wanted to do was borrow Whitney's second pencil so I could finish the test. And she/he takes the pencil and tries to hide it from me.

WHITNEY: So Blair grabs my pencil. *My* pencil . . . *(Glares at Blair, then turns back towards the audience.)* . . . and at the same time, I manage to grab the other end.

REED: Then I see them just fighting over . . . some little thing. I couldn't see what it was, but they both have one hand on it and they're pulling it back and forth.

JORDAN: I can hear them both yelling, "What are you doing?" "No what are you doing?"

BLAIR: *(Glares at Whitney for a moment, then turns back towards the audience.)* When Whitney tried to hide the pencil from me, I thought it was a joke, so I went to grab it too. I mean why would she/he not want me to finish the test? We were best friends.

WHTNEY: And Blair is yelling, "This is my pencil." And I'm yelling, "No it's my pencil." And none of it is making any sense. I mean, we were best friends.

REED: And I see them both pulling and pulling on this . . . thing.

JORDAN: And hear them both just yelling, "You let go." "No you let go." Then all of a sudden . . .

BLAIR: All of a sudden . . .

WHITNEY: All of a sudden . . .

REED: Then all of a sudden . . .

JORDAN: I have my ear up against the vent and no one is saying a thing. But there's all this heavy breathing and grunting. And then I hear a pencil snap.

(BLAIR and WHITNEY glare at each other.)

BLAIR: Whitney pulls the pencil away, says, "You want it that bad? Fine." And just breaks it in half.

WHITNEY: Blair pulls my pencil away, says, "Then no one can have it," and just breaks it in half.

REED: I see Blair and Whitney go flying apart, and I can tell that whatever this thing is just broke.

JORDAN: Then there was nothing. Just silence.

BLAIR: *(Turning back to the audience.)* I gave Whitney this look and that was it.

WHITNEY: *(Turning back to the audience.)* I never spoke to Blair again.

REED: I never saw them together again.

JORDAN: I never heard of them being friends again.

(JORDAN takes hand down from ear.)

BLAIR: *(Sadly.)*: I never spoke to Whitney again.

WHITNEY: *(Looks over at Blair. Sadly.)* My best friend.

BLAIR: *(Looks over at Whitney. Sadly.)* My best friend.

(BLAIR and WHITNEY look at each other for a moment, then turn back towards the audience.)

– END SCENE –

MEET & GREET

(Scene for one male and one female.)

(At start, LUKE and OLIVIA stand several feet apart, facing forward, towards the audience. LUKE looks at Olivia, then looks forward again before Olivia notices. OLIVIA then looks at Luke, without Luke noticing, then looks forward again. After a moment, BOTH glance over at each other. Their eyes meet for an instant, then both immediately look away again, facing forward. NOTE: Throughout most of the scene, the dialogue is strictly their inner thoughts. They are not speaking to each other.)

LUKE: OMG.

OLIVIA: OMG.

LUKE: I think that girl just looked at me.

OLIVIA: I think that boy just looked at me.

LUKE: Maybe.

OLIVIA: But did he?

LUKE: OK, I'm just gonna take one quick look.

OLIVIA: I'll just look over again for one second.

> *(BOTH simultaneously glance at each other, then immediately look away.)*

LUKE: OMG.

OLIVIA: OMG.

LUKE: She *did* look at me!

OLIVIA: He *was* looking at me!

LUKE: What should I do?

OLIVIA: What should I do?

LUKE: What should I *do*?

OLIVIA: Should I talk to him?

LUKE: I should talk to her.

OLIVIA: But what if he wasn't really looking at me?

LUKE: But what if I say something dumb?

OLIVIA: Still – everyone's always telling me to be more confident.

LUKE: I just need to think of something smart.

OLIVIA: What would a confident person say?

LUKE: What would a smart person say?

OLIVIA: And what if he says something mean back? I would totally die.

LUKE: Maybe she was just looking at my clothes – like because she hates them.

OLIVIA: Or maybe he wasn't even looking at me – like he was looking at something behind me.

(LUKE glances down at shirt.)

LUKE: But actually my clothes look pretty good today. *(Quickly smells armpit.)* And they're clean.

109

OLIVIA: But *is* he just looking behind me? *(Quickly glances behind her.)* Nah, there's nothing but a wall back there. Why would he be looking at that?

LUKE: OK, you got this. Something smart, something smart, something smart.

OLIVIA: I can do this. Confidence. Total confidence.

> *(BOTH simultaneously pause a moment, looking determined, then take a deep breath, and turn towards each other.)*

LUKE & OLIVIA: *(Simultaneously.)* Hi! *(BOTH stare at each other a moment, surprised, mouths open, then speak again. Simultaneously.)* OMG!

> *(BOTH stare at each other, not knowing what to say next.)*

– END SCENE –

KNOCK, KNOCK

(Scene for two people.)

(At start, SHAWN is inside the house. REED is standing outside, at the front door. REED knocks. SHAWN looks over at the door, frowning, not expecting anyone, and with no idea who it could be. After a moment, REED knocks again.)

SHAWN: *(Speaking through door, but not going towards it.)* Hello?

REED: Hello?

SHAWN: Hello?

REED: Hello? I'm just here to . . .

SHAWN: Who is it?

REED: I just want to . . .

SHAWN: Who are you?

REED: It's Reed. From the park.

SHAWN: From the park?

REED: Yeah, I'm the one who . . .

SHAWN: I know who you are.

REED: I just wanted to . . .

SHAWN: Go away.

REED: But I just want to . . .

SHAWN: You need to go away. Now.

REED: I just want to – those things I said.

SHAWN: What. You want to say them again?

REED: No! I want to – I want to explain.

SHAWN: I think I understood you the first time.

REED: I mean. I want to take them back. And I want to explain why I said them. Can you open the door?

SHAWN: No.

REED: Please open the door.

> *(SHAWN goes to the door and slowly opens it. REED walks in, without being asked.)*

SHAWN: I didn't say you could . . .

REED: *(Looking around.)* This is a nice house.

SHAWN: No it's not. What do you want?

REED: Well, it's nicer than mine.

SHAWN: What do you want?

REED: *(Hesitantly.)* I . . . Sometimes I see people, and they remind me of me.

SHAWN: What's that supposed to mean?

REED: I mean, I saw those kids making fun of you.

SHAWN: So you decided to help them?

REED: No. Yes. I mean, not really. They were making fun

of you for the same reasons that people always make fun of me.

SHAWN: I have no idea what you're saying.

REED: And I just thought – if I could get you to, I don't know, defend yourself, then I would know that it's possible. That when people say those things to me, *I* could maybe defend *myself*. That it's possible.

SHAWN: So you made fun of me.

REED: I wanted you to fight back. I wanted you to say the perfect thing. The thing that I could say – every time it happens to me.

SHAWN: Do you have any idea how messed up that is?

REED: I know.

SHAWN: And then you came over here.

REED: I thought . . .

SHAWN: What.

REED: I thought that . . .

SHAWN: Just say it.

REED: I thought that maybe the next best thing to knowing what to answer when people say those things to me, is . . . to hang out with someone who would never say them.

SHAWN: *(Gently.)* Cuz I know what it feels like too.

REED: Yeah.

SHAWN: *(Smiling slightly.)* Anyone ever tell you how strange you are?

REED: All the time.

SHAWN: *(Smiling a little more.)* Yeah. Me too.

> *(REED and SHAWN look at each other for a moment.)*

REED: So can I hang out for a little. See how it goes?

SHAWN: Yeah. Let's see how it goes.

> *(REED smiles for the first time.)*

REED: OK.

– END SCENE –

GOING UP

(Scene for three people.)

> *(NOTE: The entire scene takes place on an elevator and the space in front of it. At start, the stage is empty. After a few moments, MORGAN enters from stage left, pushes the "up" button, and waits for the elevator. A moment later, DEVON enters from stage right, goes to the elevator, and also stands waiting. The elevator arrives, MORGAN and DEVON get on, and MORGAN pushes a button on the panel.)*

DEVON: Can you push three?

MORGAN: *(Pushing button.)* Sure.

> *(As MORGAN and DEVON wait for the elevator doors to close, SCHUYLER comes rushing in from stage left.)*

SCHUYLER: Hold the door! Hold the door! *(MORGAN pushes the button that holds the door open. SCHUYLER enters the elevator and pushes a button.)* Thanks.

> *(MORGAN, DEVON and SCHUYLER stare straight ahead. The elevator doors close and the elevator starts to go up. Suddenly, the elevator stops.)*

DEVON: *(Nervously.)* What was that?

MORGAN : I think the elevator stopped.

SCHUYLER: The elevator definitely stopped.

DEVON: This is not good.

MORGAN: It's bad.

DEVON: Really bad.

SCHUYLER: Come on. What's the worst that could happen?

DEVON: Umm. The doors never open again.

MORGAN: And no one figures out we're in here.

DEVON: And we starve to death.

MORGAN: Or thirsty to death.

DEVON: Or wind up eating each other.

> *(MORGAN and SCHUYLER suddenly look at DEVON.)*

DEVON: *(Anxiously.)* OK, not the eating thing. I got a little carried away. But I'm totally freaking out.

SCHUYLER: Alright, my mom always says, if something goes wrong you can get worried or you can get proactive.

MORGAN: Yes!

DEVON: Definitely! . . . What does proactive mean?

SCHUYLER: It means, you do something.

DEVON: Right.

SCHUYLER: To make it better.

MORGAN: Yes! . . . Like what?

SCHUYLER: We could try pushing all the buttons.

MORGAN: OK.

(MORGAN pushes all the buttons. ALL THEE look around for several moments, waiting for something to happen.)

DEVON: Well that didn't work.

MORGAN: So what else?

SCHUYLER: What about if we all jump at the same time? *(ALL THREE look at each other, then nod.)* Ready? One.

DEVON: Two.

MORGAN: Three!

(ALL THREE jump simultaneously, then wait a moment for something to happen. Nothing happens.)

DEVON: Nothing.

SCHUYLER: *(Enthusiastically.)* Oh, I have it! *(Suddenly screaming.)* HELP! HELLLLP!

(ALL THREE start yelling for help for several moments. ALL THREE stop yelling, then wait a moment for something to happen. Nothing happens.)

DEVON: That's it. We're never getting out.

SCHUYLER: I always thought I'd live long enough to be rich.

MORGAN: Or famous.

DEVON: *(Scratching arm.)*: Or get rid of this rash. *(SCHUYLER and MORGAN look at DEVON.)* What?

(Suddenly, with a jolt, the elevator starts to move.)

SCHUYLER: Wait. What was that?

MORGAN: It's the elevator!

DEVON: It's moving!

SCHUYLER: The doors are opening!

MORGAN: Let's get out of here!

> (ALL THREE rush at the door, trying to push past each other and get out of the elevator first. ALL THREE exit elevator.)

DEVON: Wow.

SCHUYLER: Whoa.

MORGAN: Woo.

DEVON: Well, um, nice meeting you.

SCHUYLER: Yeah. I just want to get out of here.

MORGAN: Which way is out?

DEVON: It's like three floors down.

> (ALL THREE glance back at the elevator for a moment, then turn back to each other.)

SCHUYLER: Stairs.

MORGAN: Stairs.

DEVON: Stairs.

SCHUYLER: (Indicating stage left.) That way.

> (ALL THREE exit stage left.)

– END SCENE –

THE END

(Scene for two people.)

(At start, RILEY is lying on back with eyes closed. DEATH stands several feet away, watching. After a few moments, RILEY opens eyes and looks around.)

RILEY: Where am I?

DEATH: Where do you think?

RILEY: Dude, it's a simple question.

DEATH: Look around you. What do you see?

RILEY: Like, a hallway. And then kind of like a light?

DEATH: It's not a hallway.

RILEY: I think I know a hallway when I see one.

DEATH: It's not a hallway.

RILEY: Fine. Then what is it?

DEATH: It's a tunnel.

RILEY: Hallway, tunnel – whatever.

DEATH: And you know what that light at the end is?

RILEY: Like, where the tunnel ends I guess.

DEATH: You need to go to the light.

RILEY: I don't need to do anything.

DEATH: I feel like you're not getting this. *(Speaking in a spooky voice.)* Goooo to the liiight.

RILEY: Why are you using that weird voice?

DEATH: Look, I can't keep going back and forth with you. Do you need me to spell it out? I'm Death. You're dead. That's the light. And dead people go into the light. Get it?

RILEY: I mean, not really. *(Pointing in the opposite direction from "the light.")* What happens if I go *that* way?

DEATH: That's the direction you came from.

RILEY: And?

DEATH: Look, it's not complicated. You came from the land of the living. *(Points in the opposite direction from "the light.")* You died. And now you're going into the light. *(Points toward "the light.")*

RILEY: But what if I'm not ready? What if I want to go back *that* way? *(Points in the opposite direction from "the light.")*

DEATH: Back to the land of the living?

RILEY : Yeah.

DEATH : I mean, no one ever does that.

RILEY: But I could if I want to?

DEATH: I . . . I guess. Though it kind of feels like breaking the rules. And why would you want to? Everyone that shows up here just automatically starts heading to the light.

RILEY: Well, have you ever *been* to the land of the living?

DEATH: I've never really been anywhere.

RILEY: Do you want to come with me?

DEATH: *(Looking in the opposite direction from "the light.")* That way?

RILEY: Yeah.

DEATH: *(Nervously.)* I . . . I don't know.

RILEY: C'mon! You'll love it. It's really fun!

DEATH: What do you mean?

RILEY: Like, what do I mean by fun?

DEATH: I guess.

RILEY: OK, so, for instance do you guys have ice cream here?

DEATH: No.

RILEY: Parties?

DEATH: No.

RILEY: Volleyball?

DEATH: No.

RILEY : TV?

DEATH: No.

RILEY: Video games?

DEATH: No.

RILEY: Malls?

DEATH: No.

RILEY: You don't even have *malls*?

DEATH: No.

RILEY: Dude, that's it. You're coming with me.

DEATH: Away from the light?

RILEY: And into the life.

DEATH: *(Uncertainly at first, but gradually getting more excited.)* I . . . Well . . . Yeah! . . . OK!

RILEY: Cool! *(BOTH start walking in the opposite direction from "the light.")* And don't worry, we'll stop at a mall on the way out and get you a much better outfit.

DEATH: What's wrong with my outfit?

RILEY: Dude, don't get me started. And I have my mom's credit card anyway.

DEATH: Wow.

RILEY : I think you're really gonna like it out here.

(THEY exit.)

– END SCENE –

NOTES

NOTES

NOTES

DOUGLAS M. PARKER is an award-winning playwright and lyricist, as well as the author of the best-selling books *Contemporary Monologues for Young Actors, Fantasy Monologues for Young Actors, Contemporary Scenes for Young Actors* and *Contemporary Monologues for Young Actors 2.* His theatrical works include the musical, *Life on the Mississippi* (book and lyrics), based on Mark Twain's classic autobiographical coming-of-age tale; *BESSIE: The Life and Music of Bessie Smith*, based on the rise and fall of the great American blues singer; *Thicker Than Water*, a drama based on the Andrea Yates tragedy; *Declarations*, a Young Audience historical drama drawn from the letters of John and Abigail Adams from their earliest courtship through the summer of 1776; and *The Private History of a Campaign That Failed*, a Young Audience comedy based on Mark Twain's true, humorous memoir of his time as a lieutenant in the Civil War's least accomplished, most forgotten regiment. He can be reached at MonologueFrog@gmail.com.

Made in the USA
Coppell, TX
05 February 2025

45478559R10075